LIVING IN VIENNA

An International Community
of English-Speaking Women

American Women's Association of Vienna

The American Women's Association of Vienna
Singerstrasse 4/11
1010 Vienna
Austria
+43 1 966 2925
awa@awavienna.com
www.awavienna.com

CONTRIBUTORS

Editors
Wendy Williams and Laurie Richardson

Graphic Layout and Design
Ruth Loewenhardt

Copy Editors
Solmaaz Adeli, Mona Angel, Susie Bondi, Deirdre Brewster, Dagmar
Dertnig, Hilary Drake, Sheila Hargreaves, Laurel Kennedy, Susan
Richardson, Philippa Tscherkassky, Kathy Tolchinsky, Marijke van Liemt,
Pearl Williams

German Language Editor
Dagmar Dertnig

Reviewers
Bev Bachmayer, Inci Birsel, Denise Fortin, Anthea Hankey, Linda Lai,
Hannes Miklautsch, Diane Para, Stefanie Winkelbauer

Contributing Editors
Dardis McNamee, Pam Morris, Patricia Murdoch, Parisa Piramoun,
Helen Rudinsky, Linda Starodub, Mary Wagener

Advertising Managers
Dagmar Dertnig, Pearl Williams, Deirdre Brewster

Printing Managers
Pearl Williams, Brian Williams

Photographers
Jerry Barton, Ruth Loewenhardt, Lenka Peugniez, Laurie Richardson,
Philippa Tscherkassky, Mary Wagener, Wendy Williams

Acknowledgements
The editors would like to thank the members of the AWA and the many
people in Vienna's international community - in embassies, consulates,
Austrian government offices and private businesses - who provided
valuable information. The AWA would like to thank the architects Soyka /
Silber / Soyka ZT-GmbH for generously allowing the photographer
access to their construction site on Graben, which enabled the making
of the cover photo. Cover photo credit: Wendy Williams

LIV CONTRIBUTORS' COMMENTS

While reviewing a couple of chapters of LIV, I became truly impressed with the cosmopolitan worth of Vienna in this center of history and culture.

Anthea Hankey, South Africa

LIV was, quite simply, the bible, guidebook, and lifeline for my new life in Vienna decades ago, and it has continued to be a valuable helper to newcomers ever since.

Stefanie Winkelbauer, USA

Our work is done. Why wait? Fetch a copy of LIVING in VIENNA now!

Inci Bircel, Turkey

LIV has been and continues to be a fantastic resource for so many in the international community and it was a great pleasure and privilege to be part of the 2014 editing team.

Pearl Williams, USA

The LIV publication was an indispensable guide in preparing me to move to Vienna. I have recommended the book to all the newcomers I have met over the years!

Susan Richardson, USA

AWA's LIV was a lifeline for me when I first arrived in Austria. It helped me understand the delicate nuances of the Austrian people and their culture. I hope this updated edition is able to give insights into life in Vienna for newcomers and as well, serve as a daily living guide for those of us that have chosen to call Vienna home.

Ruth Loewenhardt, UK/Canada/USA

After living in Vienna for 15 years, I became editor of Living in Vienna ... and learned so much about this city! It is a wealth of valuable information.

Wendy Williams, Canada

You feel the support and dedication of the members of AWA on every page of the book. What a pity that this kind of guide doesn't exist for every city in the world - it makes an international transition so much easier.

Dagmar Dertnig, Germany

As we revised and updated this new edition of LIV, we realized how much our world has changed. Life in Vienna keeps getting better!

Laurie Richardson, USA

FROM THE U.S. AMBASSADOR TO AUSTRIA

AMBASSADOR OF THE UNITED STATES OF AMERICA
VIENNA, AUSTRIA

July 17, 2014

As the U.S. Ambassador to the Republic of Austria and the Honorary President of the AWA, I welcome you to this vibrant and beautiful city. Vienna's quaint cobbled streets, grand Baroque palaces, and luscious green surroundings combine with a great spark of energy and creativity to make it a wonderful city that I am excited to call home.

During our first year in Vienna, my family and I have started to explore the diverse range of things the city has to offer. From culture to dining, kids' activities to sports, there is so much available. *Living in Vienna* points you in the right direction for all of these, and it helps you "find your feet" for everyday challenges of life abroad.

In some ways, this move to Vienna has felt like a homecoming. My mother is from Germany and my father from Latvia, and my European heritage means many aspects of life here are familiar. Finding comfort in the familiar, excitement in the new, and enjoyment in both is what makes living in another country so special.

My family and I have enjoyed making Vienna our home over the past year. I hope you'll enjoy making it yours, as well.

Alexa L. Wesner
Ambassador of the United States of America to Austria

FROM THE MAYOR OF VIENNA

Welcome to Vienna! For many years, tourists have flocked to our city for its cultural and historic treasures, as well as its exciting urban life full of popular yearly events and festivals. As Mayor of Vienna I am particularly happy that so many guests from abroad love our city and come back to visit time and again.

Tourists and residents alike have known for many years about the famous Viennese quality of life. Vienna continues to rank among the most livable cities in the world, and again topped the "Mercer Quality of Life Survey" in 2014 – one more reason why Vienna is so attractive for the many people who come to work and live here.

The continued vitality of Vienna depends on the dedication and involvement of all the members of our community. As a center for learning, research, and innovation, the city is poised to continue to compete internationally and secure good quality of life for generations to come.

Whether you pay Vienna a short visit, stay here for a longer time, or plan to settle down, I hope you will all feel at home and that our city will find a place in your heart.

On this note, I would like to thank the American Women's Association of Vienna for their commitment and valuable work for Vienna and the Viennese. I hope that very many people will enjoy reading the new edition of *Living in Vienna* and will feel at home in our city.

Dr. Michael Häupl
Mayor and Governor of Vienna

From Our President

The American Women's Association of Vienna (AWA) is a non-profit organization with around 300 members from over 30 countries. Founded in 1924 by military and diplomatic wives to assist American women and to aid community and charitable organizations, today the AWA serves women of all nations, and continues to support the local community through philanthropic activities. Our diverse membership includes professional women, students, full-time mothers and seniors.

We provide a connection for international, Austrian and American women who live in Vienna through newcomer orientations, weekly coffees and activities, area representatives, monthly general meetings, events, newsletters, and our publication *Living in Vienna*. Our activities have a vast range; so there is certainly something of interest for everyone! You can join the book group, learn German (or improve your German), participate in the walking group, get to know Vienna's museums and architecture, meet us for a monthly Friday Night Social . . . the list goes on. AWA Vienna keeps you up to date on events happening in and around Vienna.

For over 30 years, *Living in Vienna* has been an indispensable resource for expatriates, Austrians and permanent residents alike. This updated ninth edition of *Living in Vienna* is the work of a team of talented AWA members, many of whom are professional writers and editors, who selflessly volunteered their time and talents. As a community, we appreciate their considerable efforts and thank each of them for their dedication and achievement. It is important to recognize the hard work of everyone who worked on Living in Vienna, and to individually acknowledge Wendy Williams, Laurie Richardson, Ruth Loewenhardt, Dagmar Dertnig, Bev Bachmayer, Diane Para, Pearl Williams and Deirdre Brewster for making this new edition a reality.

We hope this book will help you adapt to and enjoy this beautiful city. We encourage you to visit our website (www.awavienna.com) for more information about the AWA, and invite English-speaking women of all nationalities to join us.

Thank you for your readership.

Kathy Tolchinsky

Kathy Tolchinsky
AWA President, 2014

FROM OUR EDITORS

The American Women's Association (AWA) of Vienna was originally founded in 1924. After an inactive period during and following WWII, the AWA was re-established in 1961 and the first edition of *Living in Vienna* (LIV) was published in 1982. So there is a lot of history within the pages of this book.

Editing *Living in Vienna* is a huge undertaking that requires the dedication of a team of talented volunteers from many different countries. So there is a lot of geography and culture within this book.

As we developed this new edition of *Living in Vienna*, emailing, googling and checking social media, we saw clearly how much our world has changed since the first edition. Information and communication technologies have dramatically reshaped our lives. Yet without the conveniences of modern technology, the first members of AWA and the first editors of *Living in Vienna* created a timeless tradition of women helping women from around the world.

By carrying on the tradition of supporting the international community in Vienna, we honor the legacy of the pioneering women who founded AWA and published the many editions of this book. LIV 2014 is another milestone in the long history of AWA.

Enjoy *Living in Vienna*!

Wendy Williams & Laurie Richardson

A Special Thanks to our Advertisers

Sobolak International

Dr. Claudia Aichinger-Pfandl
Strohmayer Relocation Services
Tierklinik Döbling
Webster University

Univ. Prof. Dr. Regine Ahner
Buongustaio
Dr. Jens Busk
Cultura Wien
Dr. Gabriele Springer
Step Vienna International Relocation Services

Christ Church Vienna
Crossway International Bible Church Vienna
English-Speaking United Methodist Church of Vienna
Vienna Christian Center
Vienna Community Church

International Montessori Pre-School

TABLE OF CONTENTS

INTERNATIONAL RELOCATION

Photo Credit: Ruth Loewenhardt

1. INTERNATIONAL RELOCATION

In this chapter . . .

- Good to know . . .
- Moving: The Logistics and the Emotions
- Moving to Vienna
- 8 Top Tips for Your Move
- Moving Check List
  - At Least Three Months in Advance
  - Six Weeks Before Your Move
  - Four Weeks Before Your Move
  - Three Weeks Before Your Move
  - One to Two Weeks Before Your Move
  - Moving Day
- Moving from Austria
- International Relocation Companies
- International Relocation Glossary

Good to know . . .

You must register with the municipal office in the district where you live within three days before or after moving to a new address. Go to the District Office (*Magistratisches Bezirksamt*) for the district where you live.

Expect to experience ups and downs when you go through an international relocation. It's normal.

Use mobile devices and a wireless card because it may take a while to get an internet connection.

Open an Austrian bank account and learn how to bank online as you will need an Austrian account to set up utility services. Get a debit (ATM) card (*Bankomatkarte* or just *Bankomat*).

Check your electrical items, since many appliances will not work in another country even with a transformer or adaptor (for example, televisions from the US).

Moving: The Logistics and the Emotions

Whether you are moving to Vienna or moving away, the practical side is not very different. You need to get your paper work in order, make an inventory list, and ship the household items you want to bring with you. We have made a check list that you can use to make sure you have taken care of the most important items. While it is often easiest to focus on the practical side of a move because it is something you can control, it is also important to deal with the emotional side of an international transition.

An international move causes a sudden and immediate change in our lives. Overnight, you lose many things that mean a great deal to you and your family: your friends and perhaps family, a job, school, your neighborhood, etc. If it is your first international move, you are probably unaware of all the things that make your life meaningful. If you have moved before, you know better what to look for in Vienna.

In the practical stress of moving, many people do not take time to really say goodbye. However, to be able to get a fresh start, it is good to close what you are leaving behind. Mourning is part of this phase, and possibly even anger and sadness. You may find yourself questioning why on earth you agreed to this posting, and you might feel insecure about yourself and your future. Do not run away from these feelings; rather, acknowledge them. They give you useful information about what you need to be happy.

Once you know what has changed and how this has impacted you, you can start finding new ways to balance your life. It might be continuing your professional career, or it could be something completely different: volunteer work, going back to school, or just taking some time off for yourself. This is both the challenge and the attraction of moving.

With every move, you have the opportunity to discover and develop new talents, but you have to do it yourself! It takes energy, creativity, and courage. In this phase, you will have days when you are excited about the opportunities, and have lots of energy. And there will be moments when you feel overwhelmed, and sad about what you have given up.

It is also valuable to define yourself as a partner and a parent, and discuss this with your family. Their lives have changed, too, and they need to adapt to their new situation as well. Your kids need time to grieve and to settle in. Allow them that time, and do not push them to be "happy". As a parent, it is hard to see your children feeling sad, but like us, children need to find their new balance in this new place.

There are many good books about expatriation. *Third Culture Kids* by Ruth van Reken and David Pollock is an excellent book on internationally-mobile kids. Robin Pascoe has also written several books on moveable marriage, raising global nomads, and finally homeward bound (see www.expatexpert.com). Learning about your new host country will also help you set realistic expectations about your life there.

If you need extra support adapting to life in your new country, you can find English-speaking counselors and therapists who specialize in working with individuals and families through cross-cultural transitions.

Moving to Vienna

Some sources of helpful information:

- The website of the Austrian Foreign Ministry has information on visa and residence permit requirements: www.bmeia.gv.at/en/foreign-ministry/startpage

- You need to register (*anmelden*) in the city where you are living and get a registration certificate (*Meldezettel*): www.wien.gv.at/english/living-working/registration

  - If you rent an apartment, your landlord will have to sign the registration form, and you need to bring a copy of your rental agreement to the district office (*Bezirksamt*) where you register.

- The Vienna Expat Center can help you find answers to many questions about bureaucracy in Vienna: www.expatcenter.at

- Information on driving in Austria, including how to exchange a foreign driving license, is available here: www.help.gv.at/Portal.Node/hlpd/public/content/139/Seite.1390000

  See the **Transportation** chapter for more details.

8 Top Tips for Your Move

- Remember that each move is unique, so expect the unexpected!

- Get passport photos of you and your family members as soon as possible and keep a few copies of them in your wallet.

- Keep a copy of your *Meldezettel* with you.

- If you apply for a visa, make sure the non-working spouse and your children apply for the visa simultaneously with the working spouse.

- Your residence permit is not a substitute for your passport. You will need both your passport and your residence card when entering other countries.

- Keep valuables such as passports, cash, checks, credit cards, jewelry, original medical records, birth and marriage certificates, school reports in one place during your move and in your hand luggage while you travel. Scan important documents and make sure you have access to them.

- Don't withdraw from activities too soon. Continue to enjoy life in your place of residence for as long as possible. Maintaining a normal schedule for yourself and your children will help ensure stability. Take time to sightsee. This may be your last chance! Whether it's a museum, a park, a performance, or a nearby city, now is the time to visit.

- Separate what you need to take with you, and what will be packed. Think about the weather in the new country. Select some favorite things to create a 'home' in your temporary apartment or hotel. For kids, make sure they bring some toys to comfort them when they are sad, and to keep them busy.

Moving Check List
At Least Three Months in Advance

✓ Notify your landlord that you are leaving, check your contract for the terms of the "notice clause", details of your deposit including how to get it back, and any requirements about painting or other maintenance. If you own your home, put your house on the market for sale or to rent while you are overseas.

✓ Start doing research on your new home:
  • Look for useful websites on the internet
  • Buy a guidebook for the country and find expats who live there. Having some contacts in your new country can ease your transition. AWA can help you find friends in Vienna.
  • If you do a preview trip:
    ‣ Look at apartments and houses to get an idea of size, price, furnishings, etc.
    ‣ Visit international schools that may be suitable for your children
    ‣ Go to a supermarket to see what foods are available and get an idea of living costs
    ‣ Get to know social clubs and sports clubs

✓ Make an inventory list of the things you will bring with you (including their value for insurance) as well as what you are leaving or putting into storage.

✓ Find out about tax deductibility of your relocation expenses.

Children

✓ Discuss the move with your children and try to prepare them as much as possible. Time this discussion according to their age: older children should be informed earlier than younger children.

✓ Notify your children's school that you are leaving.

✓ Obtain any relevant documents, reports, and education records that are needed for the next school. Usually international schools require medical records and up to date vaccination records.

✓ Organize a farewell party for your children so they can say goodbye to their friends and teachers.

✓ Find out about schools in your destination country
  • Type of curriculum
  • Facilities
  • Waiting lists

Pets

✓ Decide whether to take your pets with you. The EU has clear guidelines: http://ec.europa.eu/dgs/ health_consumer/library/press/press76_en.html

✓ If you do not take your pets, start finding them a good home.

✓ As the process for taking an animal into another country can be complicated, start early to reduce any problems that may arise.

✓ Have up-to-date vaccinations, test results, health certificate, microchip and any other required information.

✓ Obtain medical records and an EU pet passport from your vet.

For more information, see the chapter *Pets*.

Passports and Visas

✓ Make sure passports are up to date with a validity date of a minimum of six months for all family members.

✓ If it is a company move, find out what paperwork is needed for the new country visa.

✓ Some countries will require that all documents are translated into the local language by a certified translator so be sure to ask which languages are accepted.

✓ If it is a personal move, research the visa application process (country government websites should have this information).

✓ Alternatively, ask your relocation agent if they offer visa assistance.

✓ Make sure you have:
  - passport copies for all family members
  - passport size photos for all family members
  - copies of birth certificates for all family members
  - copies of marriage certificate
  - medical reports (if necessary)
  - educational diplomas and degrees (if necessary)
  - residence registrations

✓ Make sure you have the necessary visas for entry into the new country for all family members.

✓ It is a good idea to have extra passport photos of you and your family for needs that may come up.

Personal Belongings

✓ Start sorting through your personal belongings, including furniture and household items, and decide what you will take with you.

✓ Buy any last minute gifts and souvenirs so they can be included in your mover's quote.

✓ It is important to consider where you are moving to when considering personal belongings. Try to find out if it is easy to buy certain items in the new country or if it would be better to buy them before you leave and include them in your shipment.

✓ Whether it is a company move or personal move, start getting quotes from moving companies. If it is a company move, you may have to present moving estimates to your company for approval before you choose a mover.

✓ If you have decided to leave some personal belongings or furniture behind, you may wish to sell them.

Your Car

✓ If you are trying to sell a vehicle before leaving, it is important to advertise it early.
  • Check that the car is in good working order and make any necessary repairs
  • Check that the paperwork is in order for selling

✓ If you sell your car in Vienna, your insurance agent (*Versicherungsberater*) can estimate a fair market value or ÖAMTC can provide a car dealer trade-in evaluation free to members, and for a minimal fee for non-members. When you sell your car, ask your insurance company for assistance in canceling your registration and returning the license plates.

✓ If you are shipping your car, gather the required documents.

✓ If you have a claim-free, clean record, ask your insurance agency to confirm your status in writing. It will help to reduce your insurance rate in the new country.

For more information, see the chapter **Banking, Taxes and Insurance**.

Moving Check List
Six Weeks Before Your Move

✓ Confirm travel arrangements to your new home.

✓ It is unlikely that you will be moving directly into your new home, so confirm temporary accommodation details. If the company is doing this for you, get as much information as possible.

✓ Visit your doctor to find out if you and your family members need vaccinations for the new country. Visit your doctors, dentist, or other medical professional to let them know you are leaving the country and obtain your medical records. Arrange for check-ups so you do not need to visit a doctor or dentist immediately in your new country.

✓ Research medical care in your destination country. Do you need medical insurance?

✓ If you already have medical insurance, will it cover you and your family in your destination country?

Moving Check List
Four Weeks Before Your Move

✓ Review the details of your move with your mover:
- Written confirmation that what you are bringing fits into your container or airfreight allowance
- Tentative delivery dates
- Up-to-date contact information and alternate contact information
- Terms of insurance
- Storage method, fees and location (if needed)
- Delivery address
- Customs requirements

✓ If you have mail delivered to your home, make sure all the necessary people are aware of your new address or give a temporary forwarding address.

✓ Make sure all your finances are in order:
- Visit the bank and arrange to cancel any bank accounts/credit cards

✓ Cancel any clubs, memberships, or subscriptions.

Moving Check List
Three Weeks Before Your Move

✓ Make sure you have contact information for all your friends.

✓ Organize a farewell party for friends and colleagues.

✓ Arrange for any special waste drop off. The Vienna locations can be found at: wien.gv.at/umwelt/ma48/ entsorgung/mistplatz/adressen.html

✓ Arrange for utilities and insurances to be stopped just before you leave and for final bills to be paid.
   - Water, Gas, and Electricity
   - Phone
   - Internet
   - Cable and Satellite
   - Cancel car insurance and try to obtain "no claims declaration" in English.

Moving Check List
One to Two Weeks Before Your Move

✓ Order any foreign currency you may need.

✓ Separate what you want to take with you and what will
   be shipped.

✓ Set up services in advance in your new country: bank
   accounts, internet access, television (if you already have
   a house or apartment).

Moving Check List
Moving Day

✓ Make sure everything is clearly labeled and ready when
   the movers arrive. Movers pack everything they see,
   unless you mark it not to be packed.

✓ Have disposable plates and beverage cups on hand to
   use after your kitchen is packed.

✓ Your goods may be in transit for up to eight or more
   weeks; plan for the interim.

✓ Mark contents on important boxes for ease when
   unpacking.

✓ When you arrive at your destination, ask the movers to
   return and pick up boxes and packing materials after
   you've unpacked. They can often reuse or recycle them.

Moving Check List
Moving from Austria

✓ When you leave Austria, you are required to cancel your
registration (*abmelden*) within three days prior to
departure. Take copies of the registration (*Meldezettel*)
of every family member to your municipal district office
and retain one for your records.

✓ If you're an Austrian or European Union citizen, find out
if you must notify the Austrian or EU authorities about
your intention to relocate.

✓ For updated information see:
www.wien.gv.at/english/living-working/registration

International Movers

Moving and storage is a competitive business. Contact several moving companies for estimates. Here are a few companies that have logistics experts familiar with regulations for international customs and security clearances. In addition to packing and moving entire households, they offer storage, and can transport smaller loads. If you aren't in a hurry to have your goods moved, ask if you can add it to a larger shipment; it can be significantly less expensive.

- A. Kühner & Sohn: www.kuehner.co.at

- Interdean International Movers: www.interdean.com

- Sobolak International Removals: http://sobolak.com

International Relocation Glossary
Documents to Bring from Home

Passport	der Reisepass
Birth certificate	die Geburtsurkunde
Marriage certificate	die Heiratsurkunde
Divorce certificate	die Scheidungsurkunde
School records/ reports	das Zeugnis
Driver's license	der Führerschein
Diploma, degree, education certificate	das Diplom, das Zeugnis
Proof of health insurance	der Krankenversicherungsnachweis
Proof of immunization	der Impfausweis

Registration and Documentation

approval, acceptance papers	der Zulassungsbescheid
change of registration	die Ummeldung
citizenship, nationality	die Staatsangehörigkeit
community, parish	die Ortsgemeinde
compulsory registration	die Meldepflicht
date of birth	das Geburtsdatum
date of issue	das Ausstellungsdatum
diploma, degrees, certificates	das Diplom, die Zeugnisse
diplomatic residency card	die Legimitationskarte
district	der Bezirk
divorce certificate	die Scheidungsurkunde
family name (print)	der Familienname (in Blockschrift)
female	weiblich
first-time application	der Erstantrag
foreign passport	der ausländischer Reisepass
gender	das Geschlecht
health certificate	das Gesundheitszeugnis
identification card for EEA & Swiss citizens	der Lichtbildausweis für EWR-Bürger

immunization record	der Impfausweis
incidental costs	die Nebenkosten
Integration Agreement	die Integrationsvereinbarung
issuing office, country	die ausstellende Behörde, Staat
labour office, employment office	der Arbeitsmarktservice (AMS)
maiden name	der Familienname vor der ersten Eheschließung
male	männlich
marriage certificate	die Heiratsurkunde
Ministry of Foreign Affairs	das Bundesministerium für Auswärtige Angelegenheiten
passport	der Reisepass
passport photos	die Passfotos
permanent residence permit	die Niederlassungsbewilligung
place of birth according to passport	der Geburtsort laut Reisedokument
postal code, zip code	die Postleitzahl
proof of language knowledge	der Sprachkenntnisnachweis
proof, certificates	die Zeugnisse
register	anmelden
register address change	ummelden

register departure	abmelden
registration form	der Meldezettel
registration office	das Meldeamt
registration of residency in	die Anmeldung der Unterkunft in
religious affiliation	das Religionsbekenntnis
re-registration, cancellation of registration in . . .	die Abmeldung der Unterkunft in
residence permit	die Aufenthaltserlaubnis
residence permit for family members	die Aufenthaltserlaubnis für Familienangehörige
signature of registration applicant	die Unterschrift der Meldepflichtigen
translator	der Übersetzer
visa	das Visum
work permit	die Arbeitserlaubnis

accident and health insurance	die Unfall- und Krankenversicherung
apartment lease (contract)	der Mietvertrag
building or house number	die Haus-Nummer
contract fee	die Vertragsvergebührung
door number	die Türnummer
down payment	die Anzahlung
electrical plug	der Stecker
electrical transformer	der Transformator
electrical utility, power authority	der Energieversorger
electricity	der Strom, die Elektrizität
extension	die Verlängerung
furnished	möbliert
furniture	die Möbel
gross rent	die Bruttomiete
guest room	das Gästezimmer
heating	die Heizung
house	das Haus
house rules	die Hausordnung
kitchen	die Küche
landlord	der Vermieter
net rent	die Nettomiete
number	die Nummer
parking permit (sticker on windshield)	das Parkpickerl

plug adaptor	der Adapterstecker
property, real estate	die Immobilie
real estate agent	der Immobilienmakler, der Makler
real estate agent's commission	die Maklerprovision
relocation	die Übersiedlung, der Umzug
rent	die Miete
repair service	der Reparaturservice
room	das Zimmer
security deposit	die Kaution
staircase	die Stiege
street	die Strasse
to rent out, lease	vermieten
to rent, hire	mieten
to search	suchen
utility and maintenance costs	die Betriebskosten
VAT (value-added-tax)	MWSt (die Mehrwertsteuer)
voltage converter (110 V to 220V)	der Spannungswandler (von 110 V auf 220 V)
water	das Wasser
yard, garden	der Garten

Relocation Services cover a broad spectrum of activity:

- Orientation
- Homesearch
- Immigration
- School and Kindergarten search
- Settle-in Service
- Departure Service
- and much more

Regardless of the problem at hand, or the challenges you may face in your new environment don't hesitate to contact us - let us help you and we'll find the perfect solution!

Moving Service:
SOBOLAK International is able to organize Moving Services worldwide.

- Door to Door Moving Services
- Packaging
- Administrative Service
- Worldwide Service
- Storage

Simply give us a call or send us an email. Whatever the query we're glad to be of assistance.

SINCE 1991

...we accompany our clients and make sure that they can dedicate themselves entirely to business, family and time off.

An employee, who doesn't need to worry about relocation, move and authority requirements, is more efficient and able to stock up energy with family and during spare time. And this is beneficial to the economy. We make sure to provide a win-win situation for everyone!

immigration **destination** departure

RELOCATION SERVICES
STROHMAYER

Concorde Business Park 1/B5, A 2320 Schwechat
Tel.: +43 1 70 621 70 Fax: +43 1 70 621 70-70
E-Mail: office@relocation-services.at
www.relocation-services.at

STEP VIENNA
Relocation Solutions Simplified

IMMIGRATION   ORIENTATION   HOUSING
REGISTRATIONS   SCHOOLING   DEPARTURE

Step Vienna is a leading provider of relocation and immigration services in Austria since 1998.

Thanks to its many years of experience, Step Vienna can focus on simplicity in all of its services.

Step Vienna
Int. Relocation Service GmbH
Head Office
Fasholdgasse 3/12
1130 Vienna, Austria

CONTACT

Tel   +43 1 897 21 54 - 0
Fax   +43 1 897 21 54 - 90
Mail   office@stepvienna.at
Web   www.stepvienna.at

VIENNA   GRAZ   SALZBURG   LINZ   VILLACH

LIFE IN AUSTRIA

Photo Credit: Lenka Peugniez

2. LIFE IN AUSTRIA

In this chapter . . .

- Good to know . . .
- At Home
- Going Out
- Getting to Know Austrians
- Greetings
- Eating and Drinking
- Tipping Guidelines
- Visiting
- Smoking
- Birthdays
- Tips for Fitting in Socially
- Tips for Fitting in at Work
- Cultural Values
- Cultural Adjustment
- Coping Mechanisms
- Life in Austria Glossary

Good to know . . .

Get informed about Austria and Vienna. Attend a cultural adaptation course if possible.

Take a German class so you feel more comfortable in Vienna. It is a good opportunity to meet other people getting to know the language and the city.

Austrians are not Germans; the two countries have very different histories and cultures.

Learn about Austrian cultural differences: Austrians tend to be more conservative, traditional and formal than many cultures. In both social and business situations, Austrians expect you to be on time. Punctuality is important.

Military time is the standard using a 24-hour clock for times. 10:00 a.m. is 1000, 10:00 p.m. is 2200, and midnight is 0000. Other time formats you may see are 17 U, 17.00, and 17 h, that all mean 5:00 p.m.

Standing single file is not customary when waiting at shops so be prepared to jostle your way in a line-up.

Austrians have a relaxed attitude toward nudity and there tends to be more nudity in the media than in most countries. There are nude beaches throughout the country, including at the ends of Danube Island (*Donauinsel*). In many pubic baths and saunas, men, women and children share the same sauna, and wear nothing but their towel. In fact, it is not permitted to wear a swimsuit in the sauna.

At Home

Austria has strict noise ordinances for apartment buildings and houses. It is a violation to make noise that can be heard outside your premises on weekdays from 2200 to 0600, and from 1300 Saturday until 0600 Monday.

Typical abbreviations in a building or elevator:

UG	*Untergeschoss*	basement or lower terrace
M	*Mezzanin*	middle floor often found in older buildings
E	*Erdgeschoss*	ground floor
OG	*Obergeschoss*	one level above the ground floor
1	**1st floor**	"2nd floor" for Americans
2	**2nd floor**	"3rd floor" for Americans
D	*Dachgeschoss*	penthouse or highest floor

Going Out

When you go out in Vienna, you will see all types of dress, but typically Austrians dress in a classic, neat and formal style. When they wear jeans, women dress them up with heels. Austrians wear sweat suits, jogging attire and tennis shoes only when participating in sports. They rarely wear shorts in the city. Lightweight pants, skirts, sundresses and capri-length pants are the norm. In general, you'll receive better service at shops if you are dressed nicely, particularly at boutiques in the 1st District.

It is customary to acknowledge shop keepers when entering a store with a simple *Grüss Gott,* and an *Auf Wiedersehen* as you leave.

You are required to carry photo ID. Austrian ID, valid driver's license, etc. is accepted, but you may want to carry your residence permit (*Aufenthaltstitel*) as your Austrian ID.

House numbers in Vienna either begin at the end of the street nearest the center of the city, or progress in a clockwise direction. However, when looking for a street address, be aware that house numbers often do not follow from one side of the street to the other. Many online maps, including those on www.wien.gv.at/stadtplan, include street numbers and public transportation routes.

You will know which district (*Bezirk*) you are in by looking at the street name and the number in front of it. The number refers to the district.

Getting to Know Austrians

Get business cards (*Visitenkarten*) printed. They come in handy when you meet new people, and when you are asked for your address in shops. It is appropriate to put your home address and home phone number on your business cards.

Greetings

When you enter a room, it is polite to greet the people that are there, whether you know them or not. The most common greeting is *Grüss Gott*. You can also say *Guten*

Morgen before noon, and *Guten Tag* any time of the day. When you leave a room, say goodbye, *Auf Wiedersehen* or *Auf Wiederschauen*. You will hear these greetings when you enter a shop, or at social function, formal dinner, reception, or classroom.

Austrians shake hands when they meet or leave acquaintances. An older person offers his hand to a younger one. A woman offers hers in return to the man's gesture. When addressing or greeting someone you've just met, look the person directly in the eye.

Eating and Drinking

In restaurants, you often seat yourself. Avoid any table marked *Reserviert* or *Stammtisch*, which is reserved for regular patrons.

Most restaurants charge for bread, rolls or pretzels that you consume from the bread basket on the table. Typically, restaurants do not serve tap water (*Leitungswasser*) with a meal unless you ask for it. In addition, if you want ice cubes (*Eiswürfel*), you'll have to ask.

Traditionally, the host of a meal or event will make a toast. Guests usually wait until he or she does before taking a drink. The host will lift their glass, make eye contact with the most senior guests and say, "*Prost!*"

When you toast someone, always look the person in the eye, and touch your glass to his lightly. Never feel obligated to drink alcohol, however. Instead, just look the person in the eye and say *Prost!*

If you invite Austrians for a meal in a restaurant, they will expect you to pay the bill. If Austrians invite you, they will pay.

Tipping Guidelines

- For waiters and taxi drivers, round up your bill by 5 or 10%. Do not leave a tip on the table in a restaurant; hand the money to your waiter.

- For porters and bellhops, tip €1 per bag.

- For repairmen, give €5 to €10, depending on the time spent and quality of the service.

- For package deliverymen, tip €1 if they climb the stairs and deliver to your door.

- For chimney sweeps, tip €1 to €2.

- For movers, give €8 to €10 per mover per day, to the crew manager to distribute.

Visiting

Invitations to private homes are rare. If you receive one, consider it an honor. Arrive promptly, dress smartly and bring a small gift for the host, hostess and children. Typical gifts include a bottle of wine or champagne, high-quality chocolates, or a small seasonal flower bouquet. (Note that chrysanthemums or white lilies are for funerals and red roses signify romance).

If you are unsure of what to wear, err on the side of formality. Women usually wear a simple dress or pantsuit; men wear a jacket and tie or a suit. Offer to remove your shoes when entering the home. Often your host will have slippers near the door, or you may bring your own. Men should always stand when a woman leaves a room or the table the first time, but not each time thereafter. It is considered polite to call the next morning to thank your host. If you are hosting a dinner or party, write detailed directions to your home, possibly with a small map, to give to people you invite. They'll appreciate it.

Smoking

Smoking is still prevalent in Austria. Although Austria has non-smoking laws, many people ignore them. Unless posted clearly that a restaurant is a smoking-only venue, all restaurants are required to have a non-smoking section. Most formal to casual sit-down restaurants in the 1st District have both a smoking and non-smoking section. You may ask those at neighboring tables to refrain from lighting up when your main course arrives. You may decline a guest's request to smoke in your home. Instead, offer your terrace or garden as an alternative.

Birthdays

Recognizing birthdays is important in Austria. You can say Happy Birthday! (*Herzlichen Glückwunsch!*) or send a card. The birthday person hosts and pays for his own celebration, which can be simple or elaborate, at a restaurant or at home.

Tips for Fitting in Socially

Do

- Address people by their formal titles and surnames (for example, Doktor Schmidt, Professor Muller) until they suggest switching to casual names.

- Knock before entering an office or other closed door.

- Wait for a mutual acquaintance to introduce you.

- Learn as much as you can about Austrian culture, especially Austria's musical heritage.

- Look a person directly in the eyes both when listening and speaking.

- Attract another person's attention by raising your index finger with your palm open and facing outward.

- Face people in the row when you pass in front of them to get to your seat in a theater.

Don't

- Speak loudly or overly effusively.

- Display affection in public.

- Interrupt when someone is speaking.

- Dress flamboyantly or scruffily.

- Keep your hands in your pockets when talking with others or when standing alone.

- Feel threatened if an Austrian moves closer to you during the course of a conversation. The Austrian concept of personal space is different.

Tips for Fitting in at Work

- Schedule appointments well in advance. If you must change it, do so as early as possible.

- Deliver well-structured presentations with detailed handouts.

- Expect some small talk before proceeding with business at meetings.

- Expect Austrians to adhere to the agenda.

- Keep the details of your private life separate from work.

- Provide business cards complete with all your titles and degrees.

- Dress conservatively.

- Expect business entertaining to be done at lunch. Wait for the host to bring up the business topic first.

- Avoid scheduling appointments between noon and 1400 or after 1700. It is common for people to end their work week as early as 1300 on Fridays so schedule appropriately. Keep in mind that many Austrians take vacation during August and the two weeks around Christmas and New Year's.

- Do not expect quick decisions. Austrians will deliberate at length before reaching decisions.

- Refrain from asking an Austrian executive about his private life.

- Do not make jokes at a formal meeting or when senior staff is present.

Cultural Adjustment

Adapting to another culture can trigger a broad range of emotions, from culture shock to exhilaration. It can be challenging at times, but it also brings rich rewards in terms of gained insight about the local culture, your home culture and you as an individual.

You can distinguish between three aspects of cultural adjustment:

- Knowledge — information about how things work
- Behavior — how you act
- Feelings — your sense of emotional well-being in the host culture

In any given situation, try to remember that you may not understand the culture and this can lead to confusion and misunderstandings. Try to consider how your behavior is perceived by the other party. What is standard behavior at home may not work in the new host environment. And remember that feeling insecure and even overwhelmed sometimes is completely normal when adjusting to a new culture.

Coping Mechanisms

For those days when it just feels like things are not working out, try some of the following:

- Be aware that you are going through a significant adjustment. Your reactions and feelings are normal.

- Set small goals. Adjusting is gradual, and things will get better with time.

- Keep a journal. Record your experiences to help you work through them.

- Take care of yourself. Get enough sleep, eat healthy food and get regular exercise.

- Pamper yourself. Write out a list of rewards for yourself and select one.

- Spend time in nature. Take a long walk with a friend.

- Build up your support network. Join in AWA activities to meet others who are adjusting. You are not alone!

- Develop your sense of adventure. Try something new: a spa, an alpine hike or cross-country skiing.

- Start new traditions such as collecting artwork or crafts by local artists.

- Keep your sense of humor!

Life in Austria Glossary

basement, lower floor	das Untergeschoss, der Keller
business card	die Visitenkarte
Cheers!	Prost!
enjoy your meal	Guten Appetit
goodbye	Auf Wiedersehen
good morning, evening	Guten Morgen, Abend
floor (of a building)	das Stockwerk
ground floor	der Erdgeschoss
Happy Birthday!	Herzlichen Glückwunsch!
identification card for foreigners	der Ausweis für Ausländer
local police	die Bezirkspolizei
reserved	Reserviert
roof terrace	die Dachterrasse
second floor (American)	der erste Stock
stand to the right, please	bitte, rechts stehen
table reserved for regular customers or for special guests of the house	der Stammtisch
top floor	das Dachgeschoss
upper floor	das Obergeschoss

First Steps in German

Photo Credit: Laurie Richardson

3. FIRST STEPS IN GERMAN

In this chapter . . .

- Good to know . . .
- Language-learning Tips
- German Language Schools
- Survival Vocabulary
- Meeting People
- Shopping
- Listen Carefully to Numbers
- Typical Terms on a German-language Form
- Time
- Spelling and the Austrian Alphabet Code
- Telephone Conversations
- "False Friends"
- German Vowel Pronunciation
- German Language Resources

Good to know . . .

Hello. Good day. (formal)	Grüss Gott! Guten Tag!
Hello. (informal)	Hallo! Servus! Grüss dich!
I am pleased to meet you.	Es freut mich, Sie kennenzulernen.

Me, too. (I am pleased to meet you, too)	Mich auch.
How are you? (formal)	Wie geht es Ihnen?
How are you? (informal)	Wie geht es dir?
I am good, I am fine thank you.	Gut, danke.
And you? (formal)	Und Ihnen?
And you? (informal)	Und dir?
I'm fine, too.	Auch gut.
Goodbye!	Auf Wiedersehen!
Bye! (informal)	Tschüss! Baba!
Have a nice weekend.	Schönes Wochenende.
Have a nice day.	Schönen Tag noch.
Thank you.	Danke.
Thank you very much.	Vielen Dank.
Thank you, you too. (formal)	Danke. Ihnen auch. (formal) Danke. Dir auch. (informal)
You're welcome.	Bitte, gerne.
Excuse me, please. Pardon me, please	Entschuldigung, bitte! Entschuldigen Sie bitte!
Excuse me? (when you did not hear what was said)	Wie bitte?
Please repeat that.	Wiederholen Sie bitte.
I am sorry.	Entschuldigung. Verzeihung.
I am sorry about that.	Es tut mir leid.

Language-learning Tips

- Get a good English-German/German-English dictionary.

- Enroll in a German language class.

- Try to speak German as often as possible, even if your vocabulary is limited.

- Watch Austrian television and listen to Austrian radio, or turn them on as "background noise." Even if you don't yet understand everything being said, you will become familiar with the rhythm and sounds of the language.

- Watch movies and favourite TV shows in German and with English subtitles if possible.

- Be patient with yourself, and be prepared to be humbled. Learning a language is hard work and it takes time.

- Some language programs offer instruction leading to the Austrian Language Diploma (*Österreichische Sprachdiplom*).

German Language Schools

Here are some of the many German language schools (*Sprachschulen für Deutsch*) in Vienna.

- ActiLingua Academy: www.actilingua.com

- Alpha Sprachinstitut Austria: www.alpha.at

- Berlitz School of Languages: www.berlitz.at

- Brainstorm: www.brainstorm.at

- Cultura Wien: www.culturawien.at

- Deutsch Akademie: www.deutschakademie.com

- Inlingua Sprachschule: www.inlingua.at

- Internationales Kulturinstitut (IKI): www.ikivienna.at

- Language Company: www.languagecompany.at

- Learn Personal: www.learn-personal.com

- Talk Partners: www.talkpartners.at

- German Courses of the University of Vienna: www.deutschkurse.univie.ac.at

- Vienna Adult Education Centers: www.vhs.at

Survival Vocabulary

Here are a few words that you may hear and see frequently. More useful vocabulary can be found throughout the chapters of this book.

Achtung!	Attention! Be careful!
der Abbruch	cancellation
Aufpassen, bitte!	Watch out, please!
der Ausgang	exit
Ausser Betrieb	out of order
das Bad	bathroom (with bathtub)
besetzt	full, no vacancies, occupied
die Bestätigung	confirmation
Betreten verboten!	No trespassing! Do not enter!
In Betrieb	working (in operation)
der Eingang	entrance
die Gefahr	danger
drücken	push
geöffnet	open
geschlossen	closed
die Korrektur	correction
links	left
rechts	right
gerade	straight ahead
die Toiletten	toilets, powder room
das WC	toilet

Vorsicht!	Danger! Be careful!
ziehen	pull

Survival Questions

I have a question.	Ich habe eine Frage.
Could you...?	Könnten Sie...?
Would you...?	Würden Sie...?
Do you have...?	Haben Sie...?
Would it be possible to...?	Wäre es möglich...?
Excuse me, where is...?	Bitte, wo finde ich ...?
the next subway stop	die nächste U-Bahn Station?
the next taxi stand	den nächsten Taxistand?
Kärntnerstrasse	die Kärntnerstrasse?

Meeting People

What's your name?	Wie heissen Sie? Wie ist Ihr Name?
Do you speak English?	Sprechen Sie Englisch?
German	Deutsch
in English	auf Englisch
I speak only a little German.	Ich spreche nur ein bisschen Deutsch.
Please speak a little more slowly. I do not understand.	Bitte sprechen Sie langsamer. Ich verstehe nicht.
Please speak German. I would like to improve my German.	Bitte sprechen Sie Deutsch mit mir. Ich möchte mein Deutsch verbessern.
Excuse me, what does this say?	Bitte, was heisst das? Was steht hier?
This says . . .	Hier steht . . .
This means . . .	Das bedeutet . . .
Where are you from? What country do you come from?	Woher kommen Sie? Aus welchem Land kommen Sie?
Where do you live?	Wo wohnen Sie?
How long will you stay here?	Wie lange bleiben Sie?
What are you doing here? Why are you here?	Was machen Sie hier?
Who are you?	Wer sind Sie?
What is this (that)?	Was ist das?
Many thanks for the invitation.	Vielen Dank für die Einladung.

Shopping

For additional words and phrases, see the chapters *Shopping and Style* and *Groceries and Gourmet*.

How much is this?	Wieviel kostet das?
Do you take credit cards?	Nehmen Sie Kreditkarten?
to pay with an ATM/debit card	mit Bankomat zahlen
price	der Preis
free	gratis, kostenlos
cheap, inexpensive	billig, günstig
expensive	teuer

Listen Carefully to Numbers

In German, you say numbers between 20 and 99 in the reverse order of how they appear on a page. For example, you write 21 in German, but you say "one-and-twenty" or *einundzwanzig*. To help you understand numbers, try writing them as you listen, and leave a space for the tens digit. When you hear 142, *einhundertzweiundvierzig*, "one hundred two and forty," write "1" for *einhundert*, leave a space, then write "2" for *zwei*, then write "4" between the two digits for *undvierzig*.

Typical Terms on a German-language Form

der Vorname	first name
der Nachname	last name, surname
der Familienname	last name, surname
die Adresse	address
die Strasse	street
die Gasse	street
der Bezirk	district
die Postleitzahl (PLZ)	postal code, zip code
das Geburtsdatum	birth date
die Staatsangehörigkeit	nationality
die Nationalität	nationality
die Auskunft	information
das Formular	form
die Unterschrift	signature
sich anmelden	to apply for, sign up, register
ausfüllen	to fill in, fill out
beantragen	to apply for
einschreiben	to apply for, sign up, register
mitbringen	to bring along, bring with
I need a form and a pen, please.	Ich brauche bitte ein Formular und einen Stift.
What do I have to enter (fill in) here?	Was muss ich hier eintragen?
Where do I have to sign?	Wo muss ich unterschreiben?
I would like to register (for a class), please.	Ich möchte mich bitte (für einen Kurs) anmelden.

Time

time	die Zeit
What time is it?	Wie spät ist es?
It's 7:00 p.m.	Es ist 19.00 Uhr.
day	der Tag
week	die Woche
month	der Monat
year	das Jahr
What year?	Welches Jahr?
date	das Datum
today	heute
tomorrow	morgen
the day after tomorrow	übermorgen
yesterday	gestern
the day before yesterday	vorgestern
this week	diese Woche
next week	nächste Woche
last week	letzte Woche
in the early morning	am Morgen
in the late morning	am Vormittag
at noon	zu Mittag
in the afternoon	am Nachmittag
in the evening	am Abend
at night	in der Nacht

Spelling and the Austrian Alphabet Code

When verbally spelling a name or address, the Austrian alphabet code is frequently used, particularly on the telephone. It is well worthwhile to learn at least the letters of your name!

A - Anton	N - Nordpol
Ä - Ärger	O - Otto
B - Berta	Ö - Österreich
C - Cäsar	P - Paula
Ch - Christine	Q - Quelle
D - Dora	R - Richard
E - Emil	S - Siegfried
F - Friedrich	Sch - Schule
G - Gustav	T - Theodor
H - Heinrich	U - Ulrich
I - Ida	Ü - Übel
J - Julius	V - Viktor
K - Konrad	W - Wilhelm
L - Ludwig	X - Xaver
M - Martha	Y - Ypsilon
	Z - Zürich

Example

If your name is "Anderson," you say, "Anton, Nordpol, Dora, Emil, Richard, Siegfried, Otto, Nordpol".

Telephone Conversations

Making a Reservation - *eine Reservierung machen*

Restaurant Hostess is A and Guest is B	
A: Restaurant "X", how can I help you?	A: Restaurant "X", was kann ich für Sie tun?
B: I would like to reserve a table for four, tonight at 1800, if possible.	B: Ich möchte bitte einen Tisch reservieren. Für vier Personen um achtzehn Uhr, wenn möglich.
A: Sure. What's your name, please?	A: Gerne. Auf welchen Namen, bitte?
B: "Greer." It's spelled "g-r-e-e-r."	B: Auf den Namen Greer. Ich buchstabiere: Gustav, Richard, Emil, Emil, Richard.
B: We have a reservation. The name is "Greer."	Wir haben reserviert. Auf den Namen Greer.

Making an Appointment - *einen Termin machen*

My name is . . . It's spelled A, N . . .	Mein Name ist . . . Ich buchstabiere: Anton, Nordpol . . .
I need an appointment, please.	Ich brauche bitte einen Termin.
on Thursday	am Donnerstag
at 1700	um 17.00 Uhr
later	später
earlier	früher

Do you have a later appointment?	Geht es auch später?
Unfortunately this is not a good time for me.	Das geht leider nicht.
Is 2:00 p.m. OK?	Passt 14.00 Uhr?
Yes, that's fine.	Ja, das passt.

"False Friends"

A "false friend" is a word that is identical or similar to a word in another language, but doesn't mean the same thing. Some of the more common English/German false friends are:

aktuell Das ist eine aktuelle Zeitung.	*current* This is a current newspaper.
also Also wir kommen dann morgen.	*so, thus, therefore* So, we're coming tomorrow.
das Argument Das ist ein gutes Argument.	*point, reasoned argument* That is a good point.
bekommen Morgen bekomme ich ein neues Auto.	*to get, receive* Tomorrow I am getting a new car.
die Milliarde eine Milliarde Euro	*billion* one billion euros
brav ein braves Kind	*good, well-behaved* a good child

der Chef Mein Chef ist sehr nett.	**boss** My boss is very nice.
dezent Die Farben sind dezent.	**unobtrusive, discreet** The color is discreet.
die Direktion Die Direktion ist gut organisiert.	**administration, management** The administration is well-organized.
eventuell Ich gehe eventuell.	**possibly, maybe** I may go. It's possible that I'll go.
das Gift Sie gab ihm Gift.	**poison** She gave him poison.
komisch Der Mann ist komisch.	**strange, odd** The man is strange.
lustig Der Film ist lustig.	**funny, amusing** The film is funny.
kurios Die Frau ist kurios.	**odd, strange** The woman is odd.
das Lokal In Wien gibt es viele nette Lokale.	**café, pub, inn** In Vienna there are many nice cafés.
das Menü Das Tagesmenü ist heute Schnitzel.	**daily special** The daily special today is Schnitzel.
die Note(n) Ich habe gute Noten in der Schule.	**grade(s)** I have good grades in school.
die Notiz(en) Ich mache mir Notizen.	**notes** I'm taking notes. I'm making a note of it.

das Objekt Dieses Objekt ist zu verkaufen.	**piece of property, house** This piece of property is for sale.
ordinär eine ordinäre Sprache	**vulgar, low, common** vulgar language
die Provision Die Provision ist zu hoch.	**commission, fee** The commission is too high.
das Publikum Das Publikum ist begeistert.	**audience** The audience is enthusiastic.
das Rezept Für dieses Medikament brauchen Sie ein Rezept.	**prescription** You need a prescription for this medication.
der Roman Der Roman ist gut.	**novel** The novel is good.
der See der Bodensee	**lake** Lake Constance
sensibel eine sensible Person	**sensitive** a sensitive person
spenden Ich spende jedes Jahr für UNICEF.	**to donate** I donate to UNICEF every year.
sympathisch Der Mann ist sympathisch.	**likable, nice, pleasant** The man is pleasant.

German Vowel Pronunciation

German has long and short vowels, and vowels with umlauts and diphthongs. Here are a few guidelines to help you pronounce German vowels.

Vowels	Pronunciation
a - Anton	[ah] "father"
e - Emil	[eh] "day"
i - Ida	[ee] "see"
o - Otto	[oh] "got"
u - Udo	[oo] "rule"

Umlauts are pronunciation symbols on vowels: a, o and u.

Umlaute	Pronunciation
ä - Ärger	[air] "hair"
ö - Österreich	[er] "fur"
ü - Übel	[yoo] "mew"

Diphthongs are two vowels together that you pronounce as one sound. When you have the vowels "i" and "e" together, you pronounce only the long sound of the second vowel, for example, you pronounce the diphthong "ei" like a long "i" sound in English.

Diphthongs	Pronunciation
eu - Leute	[oi] "oil"
au - Frau	[ow] "now"

äu - Geräusch	[oi] "oil"
ei - Ei	[i] "eye"
ie - Liebe	[ee] "see"

German Language Resources

Online translators and dictionaries are extremely helpful, however do be aware that the translations may be imprecise.

- www.translate.google.com
- www.babelfish.com
- www.dict.leo.org
- www.dict.cc

HOUSE & HOME

Photo Credit: Mary Wagener

4. HOUSE & HOME

Good to know . . .

The old and the new: older *Altbau* buildings often have three meter high ceilings, ornate wooden floors, long wooden frame windows and may have faulty plumbing. New or *Neubau* buildings usually have lower ceilings, double-paned windows, and may have better plumbing. Many top floor apartments (*Dachgeschoss*) have been renovated and are very modern with new fittings.

Measure rooms, windows, floor space and ceiling height before buying new furniture or installing old furniture. Measure the width and length of windows before buying drapery.

Purchase a shopping cart if you shop locally and are not using a car. A rolling shopping cart is a practical way to carry purchases home.

Most major furniture stores offer delivery service, installation and assembly for a fee. Many stores also rent vans and small trucks for a reasonable price.

Recycling is an important part of daily life in Vienna. For detailed information, see the Recycling section in this chapter.

Furniture

Vienna has many furniture shops and superstores with everything you will need to furnish your home and garden.

Major superstores include:

- IKEA: www.ikea.at

- Interio: www.interio.at

- Kika: www.kika.at

- Leiner: www.leiner.at

- Ludwig: www.moebel-ludwig.at

- Möbelix: www.moebelix.at

- XXXLutz: www.lutz.at

Specialty furniture shops include:

- Flamant: www.flamant.at

- KA International: www.ka-international.at

- Kraus Skandinavisk Mobelhus: www.moebel-kraus.at

- Ligne Roset: www.ligneroset.at

The Spittelberg area in the 7th District has a concentration of smaller furniture stores. Look online under *Möbel 1070 Wien*.

Antiques and Used Furniture

Vienna's rich history has left a legacy of wonderful antique furniture and has led to the development of a thriving market for old, antique and used furniture. From Baroque to farmhouse to Bauhaus, there is something to be found for any style and any price.

Some helpful antique furniture search words are:

Antiques	*Antiquitäten*
Antique Dealer	*Antiquitätenhandler*

Restoration	*Restauratoren*
Carpenter	*Tischler*
Secondhand shops	*Altwaren*

The 1st District, between Graben and the Hofburg, is home to many fine antique stores, where you can find furniture from the Viennese Secession, oil paintings, old prints, statues, jewelry, porcelain figures, old chandeliers and textiles.

Flea Markets

Churches, charities and neighborhood organizations hold flea markets (*Flohmarkt*) around Vienna. For a listing of upcoming events, see: www.flohmarkt.at/flohmaerkte/wien

At the west end of the Naschmarkt, near the U4 Kettenbrückengasse exit, there is a large flea market every Saturday from 0600 - 1200.

Auction Websites

Ebay
The online auction website offers a variety of goods and services for the household. The .at site is specific to Austria which will keep shipping costs low. The .de site includes Germany and therefore goods shipped will be more expensive. www.ebay.at and www.ebay.de

Willhaben
Willhaben, which translates to "want to have", is an Austrian

online shopping site for second-hand goods including everything from child car seats to furniture and household. If you contact the seller, you have the opportunity to see the goods before making a purchase. www.willhaben.at

Donations to Charities

Austrian charities, including Kolping and Caritas, often place donation boxes close to recycling stations and Municipal District Offices. Soft goods, clothing, bric-a-brac and book donations are welcome at thrift stores, including those at the Christ Church and the UN Women's Guild.

- Christ Church Shop: www.christchurchvienna.org

- Kost Nix Laden: www.umsonstladen.at

- United Nations Women's Guild: www.iaea.org/unwg

Drapery and Upholstery

If you need draperies made, chairs upholstered, or want to purchase furniture with your choice of fabrics, these stores offer fabrics and upholstering.

- Backhausen: www.backhausen.at

- Texx Factory Outlet: www.texx.cc

- KA International: www.ka-international.at

- Les Tissus Colbert: www.lestissuscolbert.com

- Staltner & Füerlinger: www.staltner.at

- Textil Müller: www.textil-mueller.at

Household Electronics and Appliances

Vienna has many large stores that sell competitively-priced home appliances, TVs, stereos, computers and notebooks, photo equipment and printers. The following stores have several locations throughout Vienna:

- Media Markt: www.mediamarkt.at

- Saturn: www.saturn.at

- Niedermeyer: www.niedermeyer.at

- Interspar: www.interspar.at

Comparing Prices

Geizhals, which means "cheapskate", provides price comparisons. On this website, you enter the brand and model number of a product, and it will generate a list of stores and comparative prices. www.geizhals.at

Manuals, Warranties & Repairs

Many appliances come with user manuals and operating instructions in multiple languages, including English. If yours doesn't, go to the manufacturer's website where you often can download the instructions in English.

Austrian law extends warranties on electrical appliances to two years. Keep your receipt as proof of the date of purchase.

If you need repair of a major appliance during the warranty period, a repairman comes to your home and services the machine. Even if they find nothing wrong, there will be a service charge.

If possible, take an out-of-warranty appliance to a designated service center instead of to the store where you bought it. Although the store may handle repairs, it can be expensive, and replacement or service can take a long time. When buying a new machine, ask if the store will be responsible for the installation and warranty; in general, they are not included in the purchase price.

Lighting

In addition to neighborhood lighting shops, most major household and department stores sell lighting. Home electronics and DIY stores also have a large selection of lamps and lighting. Search online under *Beleuchtung* or *Lampen in Wien*. Amazon.de and other online shops are also a good source for finding lighting.

Vienna homes tend to use more wall and ceiling fixtures than lamps, and often there are few electrical outlets. If you need to install lights, ask your landlord to share the cost in exchange for leaving the lighting behind when you move out. Lamps from other countries will work with a change of bulb and plug adaptor.

Fluorescent Tube Recycling

When you purchase a fluorescent tube, the price includes a deposit. Return your burned-out tubes to a lighting store to receive a refund of your deposit.

Keys

Every security key is registered to the owner of an apartment or house. A locksmith will not duplicate a security key without the permission of the apartment or house owner. The typical cost of a replacement key is €50.

If you find yourself locked out (*ausgesperrt*), look online for a nearby locksmith who makes emergency keys. Search for *Ausperrdienst* and the district where you live.

Replacing keys can be very expensive. If you lose a key, you need to file a police report. If you do not report the loss and your apartment or house is burgled without forced entry, your insurance will not cover the loss. If the lost key permits entry to your building, you may have to pay to replace the entry lock and pay for new keys for others in the building. If you lose the key to a security door, getting in to your own home will be costly. If you leave a key in the lock on the inside of the door, it blocks the key opening from the outside. If you have children, consider replacing an inside keyhole with a locking knob instead, or replacing it with a double cylinder. For assistance, see: www.sicherheitstechnik-nitsch.com

For added protection, you can register your keys:

Key Return Center
Schlüsselfundzentral
You receive a metal tag to put on your key ring asking a finder to take the found keys to the Municipal District Office. The Return Center will call you and pay a reward to the finder. English is spoken. www.schluesselfundzentrale.at

Home Services and Care

If you are renting an apartment or house, you are responsible for routine maintenance and costs of heating, electricity and plumbing. Read your lease carefully, or have someone explain your obligations.

When you move in, ask your landlord or building superintendent (*Hauswart*, *Hausmeister* or *Hausbesorger*) for the name and telephone number of a plumber, an electrician and a heating specialist.

Heating Inspection

You are required to have your furnace inspected annually. You must show the inspection receipts when you vacate the apartment. Check the brand name of the furnace and then find the appropriate service center in your area.

Chimney Sweeps

At least once a year, a chimney sweep (*Rauchfangkehrer*) will come to your home to check fireplaces, water heaters, and combination boilers. Usually the chimney sweep will post the day and time of his visit in your apartment building in advance of his visit. Someone must be in your residence to admit him, unless you arrange an alternate time. See the Vienna *Rauchfangkehrern* website for further information: www.wienerrauchfangkehrer.at

Handyman and Home Repairs

Items in your home may need professional cleaning or repair. Labor costs are usually by the hour, and travel time is additional. If possible, obtain a written estimate before work begins.

There are two types of estimates: binding or guaranteed cost estimate (*verbindliche Kostenvoranschlag*) or non-binding cost estimate (*unverbindlicher Kostenvoranschlag*). If you have a binding estimate, you pay the amount of the estimate, regardless of the actual repair cost. If you have a non-binding estimate, you must pay the actual repair price, up to 15% above the estimated cost. If the costs will be higher, the repairer must inform you. You can terminate the agreement, but you are obligated to pay for services rendered to date.

If you need a carpenter, electrician or other craftsman, word of mouth is the best source for finding reliable help. Churches, international organizations and grocery stores often have bulletin boards listing English-speaking handymen. Always use a licensed specialist who is knowledgeable about Austrian codes for electrical and plumbing installation and repairs.

Appliance Repairs

The cost to repair out-of-warranty small appliances (*Elektrogerätereparatur*) often exceeds the replacement cost. If you want to have an item repaired, get an estimate in writing. Quality brands such as Philips, Miele, and Siemens have their own repair services. Search for Customer Service (*Kundendienst*) on the manufacturer's website. Some electrical appliance stores also offer repairs and service.

You usually pay a minimum of €50 to have a repairman come to your home. Even if your appliance is not repaired, you must still pay this fee. Cost estimates are free, unless stated otherwise in advance.

Fabric Care

Bedspreads, comforters or large throw rugs are typically too big to clean in a standard European home washing machine. Overloading a front-loading machine may result in an expensive repair bill. Take large items to a laundromat or have them washed or dry cleaned professionally.

Laundromats

Most apartment buildings have washing machines for the use of residents, however clothes dryers are not common. There are laundry facilities with coin-operated washers and dryers (*Münzwäscherei*) in several Vienna neighborhoods. Bring plenty of one euro coins. Although some laundromats include detergent in the price of a wash, you may want to bring your own detergent, especially when washing colored or dark clothing. If you think you can't live without your favorite detergent from your home country, remember that European detergents are formulated to accommodate the hardness of the local water.

Dry Cleaning

Dry cleaning can be expensive. Expect to pay €10 to clean a two-piece suit and at least €2 for a man's shirt.

Clothes Washing

European front-loading washing machines tend to have long wash cycles. There are many combinations of temperature, spin speed, and length of washing cycle. Here are a few guidelines:

Synthetics and permanent press clothing (*Pflegeleicht*)	30° or 40°
Cottons (*Baumwolle*)	most wash well at 30° or 40°
To sanitize towels, sheets, or other sturdy fabrics, use the highest temperature on your machine. Austrians call this cycle *Kochwasche* which literally means to cook the wash.	usually 95°
Delicates and washable wools (*Feinwasche*)	30° or cooler on the Delicate or Handwash cycle

When you close the door of a front-loading washing machine and start the washer, the door locks. Usually you cannot open the door to add or remove items unless you cancel the wash cycle. At the end of a cycle, or during a power failure, the washing machine door remains locked for up to a minute.

Clothes Drying

Space restrictions and energy costs make a clothes dryer a luxury for many Europeans. Even if you have one, you may want to purchase a sturdy drying rack to hang damp or wet items.

If you can accommodate a dryer but don't have a location for the external exhaust, you can buy a condensation dryer, which collects the condensed water from your clothes as they dry. You empty the container after each load, or more frequently when drying very wet articles.

You can buy a combination washer-dryer that offers the convenience of one appliance, but won't dry your clothes completely, and tend to take a very long time: two hours or longer to wash and dry one small load of laundry.

If your apartment comes with a washing machine, check its age and get a guarantee that it will be repaired or replaced by the owner.

Beds and Bed Linens

Austrian bedding include a fitted sheet (*Spannleintuch*) covering the mattress, topped by a down comforter (*Bettdecke*) inside a washable cover (*Überzug*). Bed linens are usually sold in sets of a comforter cover and a pillowcase. Fitted sheets are sold separately.

All major household and department stores have linen departments and specialty shops offer high-end linens. Search under *Bettwaesche Wien* to find a store in your neighborhood. Be aware of bed sizes, which may be different from your home country. Use these measurements as a guide:

Standard Austrian Mattress Sizes

Bed Size	German	Size (centimeters)
Single or Twin	*Einzelbett*	90 x 200
Double	*Dobbelbett*	140 x 200
Queen*	*Dobbelbett 160*	160 x 200
King*	*Dobbelbett 180*	180 x 200

*Queen and king size beds are usually two single mattresses side-by-side.

Comforters

Most bed covers (*Bettdecke*) are 140 cm x 200 cm. Queen and king size beds will usually have two single comforters.

Storage

Your apartment may have limited space or your basement (*Keller*) may be too damp for storage. You can rent extra storage space from several self-storage companies offering clean, dry, accessible storage facilities. There are many locations in and around Vienna, including climate- and humidity-controlled rooms for wine storage.

Domestic Help

The best way to find domestic help is via word of mouth and recommendations from members of international clubs such as AWA. Your local grocery store may also have a notice board where you can find help or post an advertisement. Be sure to request references.

The current hourly rate for domestic help is about €10, plus transportation costs. It is customary to provide lunch for a full day of work.

If you employ a domestic, you are responsible for paying contributions to the national health insurance and retirement funds. The amount changes every calendar year. Make sure that your employee registers with the Chamber for Workers and Employees (*Kammer für Arbeiter und Angestellte* or *Arbeiterkammer*).

Hardware and DIY

Vienna still has small, independent hardware stores. Check online under *Eisenwaren* or *Eisenhandlung* and include "Wien" and your postal code to locate a store near you.

There are several large DIY chains that often have a garden center and greenhouse.

- OBI: www.obi.at

- Hornbach: www.hornbach.at

- Bauhaus: www.bauhaus.at

- BauMax/Mega-Baumax: www.baumax.at

Garden Centers

Austrians are enthusiastic gardeners, and garden centers and flower shops abound throughout the city. Grocery stores also have selections of cut flowers.

The major gardening centers are:

- Bellaflora: www.bellaflora.at

- Dehner Gartencenter: www.dehner.at

- Gärtner Starkl: www.starkl.at

Recycling

Large recycling containers or dumpsters are either in your apartment building or neighborhood. All are clearly marked according to waste category: paper, plastic bottles, clear and colored glass, metal cans, and biodegradable material. For details on recycling, see: www.wien.gv.at/umwelt/ma48/beratung/muelltrennung/index.html

Tetrapaks

You can recycle your empty wax-coated milk and juice containers called Tetrapaks. Öko-Box cartons are available at your local grocery store. Fold the cartons flat and leave them outside for pick-up on the day indicated on the box. For more information, see: www.oekobox.at

Batteries

Recycling boxes for used batteries are located at electrical appliance stores and grocery stores near the cashiers. There are also hazardous waste drop-off points (see below).

Bulk and Hazardous Waste

Dispose of large recyclables, hazardous waste and bulk waste at designated recycling and disposal centers (*Mistplätze*). Bulk waste includes any trash that is too large for regular garbage bins. Electronics and appliances also require special disposal. Recycling and waste disposal centers are located throughout Vienna. Hours are generally Monday to Saturday 0700-1800. For details, see: www.wien.gv.at/umwelt/ma48/entsorgung/mistplatz/index.html

Hazardous waste (*Problemstoff*) includes car oils, pharmaceutical drugs, paints, battery acids or any substance that can endanger human, plant or animal life. Use this link for more info on hazard waste and how to dispose of it: http://www.wien.gv.at/umwelt/ma48/beratung/muelltrennung/problemstoffe.html

There are also mobile collection sites for hazardous waste: http://www.wien.gv.at/umwelt/ma48/entsorgung/problemstoffsammlung/mobile-prosa-sammeltermine.html

Bulk Trash Pick-up

The city will pick up household furniture or large items for recycling, including refrigerators, for a fee. Information is available at: www.wien.gv.at/umwelt/ma48/entsorgung/ entruempelung.html

House and Home Glossary

Do you accept credit cards?	Nehmen Sie Kreditkarten?
Do you do home delivery?	Können Sie nach Hause liefern?
Do you offer installation?	Bieten Sie Montageservice an?
How much does this cost?	Wieviel kostet das?
What is the fee for this service?	Wieviel kostet dieser Service?
When can I expect delivery?	Wann kommt die Lieferung?
Where can I find . . .?	Wo finde ich bitte . . .?
advice	der Ratschlag
all-purpose cleaner	der Allzweckreiniger
ammonia	der Salmiakgeist
antiques	die Antiquitäten
appliances	die Geräte
armchair	der Sessel
armoire, wardrobe	der Schrank
bath	das Bad
bath mat	die Badematte
bathroom	das Badezimmer
bath towel	das Badetuch
beach towel	das Strandtuch
bed, bed frame	das Bett, das Bettgestell
bedding, linens	die Bettwäsche

bedroom	das Schlafzimmer
bedspread	die Überdecke
blanket	die Decke
bleach	das Bleichmittel, der Entfärber
blinds	die Fensterläden, die Jalousien
bookcase	das Bücherregal
bouquet	der Blumenstrauss
boxed shirts	die zusammengelegten Hemden
buffet, sideboard	die Anrichte
building materials	die Baustoffe
carpet	der Teppich
ceramic tile cleaner	der Fliesenreiniger
ceramic tile	die (Keramik) Fliese
chair	der Stuhl, der Sessel
chair cushion	das Sitzkissen
chimney sweep	der Rauchfangkehrer
cleaning products	die Reinigungsprodukte
cleaning	die Reinigung
coin-operated washing machine	die Münzwaschmaschine
comforter	die Bettdecke, das Federbett
comforter cleaning	die Bettfedernreinigung
concierge	der Hauswart
corrosive	ätzend

couch	die Couch
curtain rods	die Vorhangstangen
curtains, drapery	die Vorhänge, die Gardinen
desk	der Schreibtisch
detergent	das Waschmittel
dining room	das Esszimmer
discount	der Rabatt
dishwasher detergent	das Geschirrspülmittel
dishwasher salt	das Geschirrspülsalz
drain cleaner	der Abflussreiniger
dress	das Kleid
dresser	der Schrank, Kleiderschrank; die Kommode
dry cleaner	die Reinigung
duvet cover	der überzug
duvet	die Federdecke
emergency lock service	der Aufsperrdienst
entertainment center	das Unterhaltungszentrum
environmentally-friendly	umweltfreundlich
fabric	der Stoff
fabric softener	der Weichspüler
fitted sheets	die Spannleintücher
flammable	brennbar
flooring	der Fussboden
florist	die Blumenladen
flower	die Blume
folded shirts	gefaltete Hemden

furniture dealer	der Möbelhändler
furniture store	das Einrichtungshaus
furniture	die Möbel
garden	der Garten
gardener	der Gärtner
garden furniture	die Gartenmöbel
gardening	die Gartenarbeit
garden tools	die Gartengeräte
hand towel	das Handtuch
hanger	der Kleiderbügel
highly toxic	hoch giftig
hobbyist	der Bastler
ironing	das Bügeln
irritant	gesundheitsschädigend
jacket	die Jacke
key	der Schlüssel
kitchen	die Küche
kitchen equipment	die Küchengeräte
lamps	die Lampen
lampshade	der Lampenschirm
laundromat	der Waschsalon
laundry (clothing)	die Wäsche
laundry (commercial)	die Putzerei
laundry room	die Waschküche
light bulb	die Glühbirne
lighting	die Beleuchtung

lights	die Lampen, die Lichter
living room	das Wohnzimmer
lock	das Schloss
locksmith	der Schlüsseldienst
lost key service	die Schlüsselfundzentrale
mattress cover	der Matratzenschoner
mattress	die Matratze
mirror	der Spiegel
nails	die Nägel
napkin	die Serviette
necktie	die Krawatte
nursery (for plants)	die Gärtnerei
office	das Büro
paint stripper	der Abbeizer
paint	die Farbe
painting	das Bild, das Gemälde
pants, trousers	die Hose
parquet	das Parkett
pillowcases	die Polsterüberzüge, die Bezüge
pillows	die Polster, die Kissen
planter	der Blumentopf
plants	die Pflanzen
potting soil	die Blumenerde
quilt	die Steppdecke
repair	die Reparatur
roller shade	das Rollo

rug	der Teppich
screws	die Schrauben
seeds	die Samen
sheets	die Leintücher
shelves	die Regale
shirt	das Hemd
shower curtain	der Duschvorhang
showroom	der Ausstellungsraum
skirt	der Rock
slacks	die Freizeithose
stain removers	der Fleckenentferner
stains, spots	die Flecken
starch	die Stärke
suit	der Anzug
table	der Tisch
table lamp	die Tischlampe
table linens	die Tischwäsche
tablecloth	das Tischtuch
tea towel	das Geschirrtuch
tools	die Werkzeuge
travel time (for repair services)	die Wegzeit
TV stand	der Fernsehtisch
unlocked	aufgesperrt
upholstered furniture	die Polstermöbel
upholstery	die Polsterei
upholstery cleaning	die Polstermöbelreinigung

upholstery fabric	der Bezugsstoff
walk-in closet	der begehbare Schrank
wall light	die Wandleuchte
wallpaper	die Tapeten
wallpaper hanger	der Tapezierer
warnings	die Warnleuchte
washcloth	der Waschlappen
window cleaner	der Fensterreiniger
wood floor cleaner	der Parkettreiniger

Communication

Photo Credit: Jerry Barton

5. COMMUNICATION

Good to know . . .

Electrical equipment operates on 220V 50Hz. Most televisions from outside continental Europe do not work in Vienna. For DVD players, you need zone 2 (Europe) or code-free (unrestricted).

With a prepaid SIM card and an unlocked cell phone, you can have phone service with a service provider without a contract.

Ask about cell phone and television reception in your neighborhood. Check with your building superintendent or neighbors, or contact a service vendor for advice on which cell phone, internet and television options are best for you.

Confirm that you can get support in English before you sign a contract with a service provider. Also check that your contract is valid if you move during the guarantee period.

In Austria you must pay a television and radio fee (*Rundfunkgebühr*), which subsidizes the radio and television programming of the public broadcaster ORF (Austrian Public Radio and Television). Even if you don't watch or listen to ORF programming, you must register and pay the annual fee. For information: www.gis.at/sprachmenu/english

Technology changes rapidly. Austria is a world leader in telecommunications and emerging services, giving you access to cutting-edge technology. It also means that you have many options to choose from, which can make it a challenge to find the best deal for your specific needs.

Living in Vienna does not recommend any provider or technology. The information in this chapter represents our best efforts to provide you with up-to-date details about the services available at the time of publication.

Communication Packages

A simple option is to have a single company provide all services: fixed-line, cell phone, internet, cable, digital television and other media needs. The main providers are:

- Telekom Austria: www.a1.net
- UPC Telekabel: www.upc.at

Fixed-line Telephone Service

In Austria, usually you pay for every call that you make from your fixed-line phone (*Festnetz*). However, you can subscribe to a flat-rate package, including discounted rates for international calls. Here are two main fixed-line providers.

- Telekom Austria: www.a1.net
- Tele2: www.tele2.at

Cell Phone Signal

Before you buy or rent a cell phone or set up a wireless internet connection, make sure the signal in your area is strong enough to support it. Signal strength varies from place to place, even within the same district. Be aware of roaming fees; connections become costly when you move outside the area.

US Cell Phone Compatibility

If you purchase a cell phone in the US, it will work in Europe if it is a 3G phone. However, be aware that your US phone will not work with a European SIM card for three months after the purchase date.

Cell Phone Service

You pay only for outgoing calls on your cell phone. If you don't make many calls, it may be less expensive to use a cell phone rather than a fixed-line. There are several cell phone service providers in Austria, including A1, One, T-Mobile and Telering. Rates and services change frequently. If you switch providers, you have the right to take your number with you.

If you want a cell phone for only a limited time, try Bob or Yesss, or one of the many other prepaid cell phone services. Initial costs are about €15 if you have a compatible cell phone. For more information, see www.bob.at and www.yesss.at

Providers lock their phones, but you can unlock them yourself by entering a code on the touchpad, or have them unlocked for a fee at one of the many cell phone shops throughout the city. Many websites explain how to unlock a cell phone, including www.thetravelinsider.info

Free Communication Services

You may use your desktop, tablet computer or smart phone and software or Apps such as Skype or Yesss, to connect. This is a popular and inexpensive or free way to speak with one or many people around the corner or around the world. If you call computer-to-computer, you pay nothing; if you call a fixed-line telephone, you pay a few cents per minute. There are also services that enable you to make overseas cell phone-to-cell phone calls at local rates.
Note that online communication providers such as Skype do not support toll-free or emergency service numbers.

Radio

There is no English-language radio station in Vienna. However, there are a few broadcasts in English:

- Ö1 (92 MHz) weekdays at 0800: news in German, English and French

- FM4 (103.8 MHz) Mon - Fri 0600 - 1000: youth-oriented programming, music and news in English, news in English throughout the day

If you want to listen to your favorite radio station from home, try internet radio, webcasts and audio streaming. Look up the radio station website of your favorite program, and you may be able to listen to broadcasts on your computer. Some programs offer free podcasts that you can download.

Television

Before you decide on the television service you want, find out from your landlord if the property has cable or satellite connections. If not, you may have to arrange for installation and wiring.

Cable TV

Currently UPC Telekabel, the local cable company, offers four English-language channels:

- CNBC International
- CNN International

- BBC Entertainment
- BBC World

Satellite TV

Satellite television brings hundreds of channels, including a large selection of English-language programming, into your home. To install a satellite dish at your apartment, you must first have permission from your landlord. If your house or apartment building has a satellite dish, you need a satellite receiver for reception. If your apartment has its own dish, you may be able to choose from among different satellite companies' offerings.

German-language Television

There are so many ways to access English programs and movies that it is easy to avoid German-language television. However, watching German-language television is a good way to improve your German while learning about Vienna, Austria, Germany and Switzerland. Many programs you know from your home country may be shown dubbed or subtitled in German; you may even find a new local favorite. News programs are a great place to start because newscasters tend to speak German clearly and without dialect. You can find many shows, including national news programs, broadcast with subtitles in German or other languages. Check the Teletext pages of the station for details.

Media Downloads

iTunes is one of many places to download music, movies, audio books and television programs onto a computer, tablet or smartphone. A growing collection of movies is available for purchase or rental, and you can buy classic and current television programs. Be aware that your selection may be limited to programs available only to Austrian customers, especially if your payment method billing address is in Austria.

Other TV Alternatives

Some expatriates in Vienna report success watching television programs from their home country on their computer or cell phone using Slingbox. You can stream a program from a set-top box or digital video recorder located in your home country directly over the internet to a computer or other web-connected device. There is no service fee, but you need to buy a Slingbox device, which is available in the US and in a handful of European countries. For more information, see www. slingbox.com.

Computers

If you bring a computer from abroad, you will need an end-of-plug adaptor. Check that your computer's power supply adapts to the local voltage, which is 230V 50Hz. Check, too, that any printer you want to bring with you operates at this voltage. If your printer runs only on 110V, you will need a voltage converter to use it in Vienna.

Computer Purchases

Off-the-shelf computers sold in Austria have a German keyboard and operating system. If you want these in English, ask your dealer if he can order them for you.

If you will be writing documents in German, it can be handy to have the German keyboard and vowel keys with umlauts. If you "hunt and peck", you will find all the necessary letters and symbols to type in English. If you touch type, you can set English as an operating system language in your software setup. You can toggle between the two keyboard layouts.

You can install and run software in any language on a computer you buy in Austria.

IT Assistance

Many guarantees and service contracts do not cover products outside the country where they were purchased. Before you move, check to see if you can buy a worldwide policy. Most stores that sell computers also offer repairs. For more information, search for *Computer Reparatur und Service*.

Internet Connections

Several internet connection options are available in Vienna.

DSL operates over the telephone line. You can subscribe to a package for a fixed-rate monthly fee and a specific data download limit. You need an installed telephone line and a modem, which usually can be installed with technical support from the service provider. Additional fees may apply if your internet service provider is not Telekom Austria or another company which has an agreement with them to use their lines.

Cable service is similar to DSL service, but operates over your existing television cable connection. Service is provided through your cable company.

Mobile internet is simply the internet through cell phone signals. It allows you to access the internet with your laptop without searching for a hotspot or purchasing a wireless router for your home. Austria has one of the best-covered and fastest 3G wireless networks in the world. Contracts are with cell phone operators who provide a special SIM card and a modem that you connect to your laptop. In general, A1 and T-Mobile have good coverage. The company "Drei" also offer wireless internet. Verify coverage in your area.

Using mobile internet outside of Austria can be expensive if you don't have a data roaming plan. Even with such a plan, roaming is costly.

Internet Service Providers (ISPs)

There are a number of companies that provide internet services. Not all ISPs have English-speaking assistance; you may need a German speaker to help you communicate with the customer support staff.

The amount of data you can upload and download from the internet may be limited by your DSL, cable, and wireless internet contracts. You may have an unpleasant surprise and a high bill if you exceed the quantity allowed in your package. The main ISPs in Austria are:

- Chello/UPC Telekabel Wien: www.upc.at

- A1 Telekom Austria: www.a1.net
- Tele2: www.tele2.at

Wireless Routers

You can buy a wireless router for a PC for about €75 and, using your provider's modem, establish a wireless network in your home that can be accessed by multiple users. You will want to secure your network with a password so that unauthorized users cannot access it. If you're a Mac user, all Apple Airport products work in Austria.

Wireless LANs (Wi-Fi)

There are many places in Vienna where you can connect wirelessly for free, or for a minimal charge, including many hotels, cafés, businesses, schools and public buildings. To access the system at some locations you need to ask the store manager or café waiter for the network password.

Mail Services

- City maps indicate the location of post offices with the Post symbol

  Post

- Post office hours are usually Monday to Friday 0800-1800

- Main Post Office (*das Hauptpostamt*) 1, Fleischmarkt 19 is open every day of the year, Monday to Friday 0700 - 2200, Saturday and Sunday 0900 – 2200

Post Office Locations

To find the location and opening hours of your local post office, go to www.post.at. Change the language to English and under "Branch Locator" type your four-digit postal code. The list will show you all branches in your district. To see the office's opening hours, click *Öffnungszeiten*.

Mail Delivery

* Your mail carrier (*Briefträger*) delivers mail from Monday to Friday unless it is special delivery mail.

* To ensure that letters and packages reach you quickly from outside Austria, ask the sender to address them like this:

> Name
> Street Name and House Number/Staircase/Apartment
> Postal Code and City
> Austria

* The second and third numbers in your postal code indicate the district (*Bezirk*) where you live in Vienna. **10**10 indicates the 1st district; **11**90 is the 19th.

* If you are not home to receive a package or letter, your mail carrier will leave a yellow receipt (*Benachrichtigung*) in your mailbox. To pick up the item, take the receipt and a photo ID (*Ausweis*) to the location indicated. If the letter is registered (*eingeschrieben*), only the addressee can claim it.

- Mailboxes are yellow and often mounted on buildings. Pick-up times are posted on the front of the mailbox.

Mail Hold

- If you are away or unable to access your mailbox for a week or longer, you can arrange for a mail hold (*Urlaubsfach*) at your local post office for a fee.

- You can arrange for a mail hold at any post office in the city, but you need to know the exact location of your local branch where your mail will be held, and you must present a photo ID. When you return, pick up your mail in person from the post office. Take a photo ID and your mail-hold receipt with you.

Forwarding Order

If you want your mail forwarded to another address, you can arrange for a forwarding order (*Nachsendeauftrag*) at your post office. You can use this service to forward mail temporarily to your vacation address, or to forward it permanently to your new address, inside or outside of Austria. There is a nominal fee for the first three months, and an additional fee for each subsequent three-month period. Be aware that you may have to pay additional per-item postage to have magazines, newspapers and packages forwarded outside of Austria.

Package Pickup

Several post offices offer an automated service called Post. 24 where you can pick up packages 24 hours a day. A sender (in Austria only) addresses your package to a Post. 24 station, giving your cell phone number or email address. When your package arrives at the Post.24 location, you receive a text message or an e-mail with a pick-up code.

Junk Mail

If you do not want to receive unsolicited mail, you can attach a sticker *Bitte keine Reklame* (Please No Advertisements) to your mailbox. You can get free stickers at the post office or by sending a self-addressed, stamped envelope to:

> Bitte Keine Reklame
> Postfach 500
> 1230 Wien

Postal Rates

The post office has different rates for letters (up to 2,000 grams) sent within Austria and those mailed worldwide. You can send letters and small packages either priority or economy, overnight express mail (EMS) domestically and internationally. EMS mail usually takes 1-3 days anywhere in the world.

You can find rates (*Postgebühren*) for letters and packages online: www.post.at/en/personal_sending.php1

Depending on the location of the addressee, you may have to fill out a postal form (*Aufgabeschein* or *Zollerklärung*) to mail a letter or package.

Sending Packages

You can send a small package (*Päckchen*) or a large parcel (*Paket*) up to 31.5 kg from any post office. You can also send small packages overnight express mail domestically and internationally.

Other Delivery Services

The main international delivery services in Vienna:

- DHL Express: www.dhl.at
- FedEx: www.fedex.com/at_english
- UPS: www.ups.com
- Mail Boxes Etc.: www.mbe.at
- ÖBB Rail Cargo: www.railcargo.at/en/

A couple of tips before you send your package:

- Check with each carrier before taking a package for shipment; there may be limits on size and weight, and some destinations require customs declarations. A limit of 20 - 30 kilos is common. Be aware that the recipient of the package may have to pay customs duties.

- There are many local courier services (*Botendienst*). For shipping large items by air, consider airfreight or extra baggage, and call ahead to make arrangements. For shipping by land, an expeditor or moving company may be your best option. The Austrian National Railroad (*ÖBB*) also offers a variety of rail cargo services.

Forwarding Agents

Usually you do not need a forwarding agent *(Spedition)* within Austria or the European Union. However, for all other regions, you may want someone to handle your shipment. Here are two agents:

- DPD: www.dpd.at
- GLS: www.gls-group.eu

Communication Glossary

address	die Anschrift
addressee	der Empfänger
air mail	die Luftpost
amount to be collected on delivery	der Nachnahmebetrag
bank ID number	die Bankverbindung, die Bankleitzahl
broadcast fee	die Rundfunkgebühr
by air	auf dem Luftweg
by the most economical way	auf dem preisgünstigsten Weg
cash on delivery (COD)	die Nachnahme
cell phone	das Handy
change of address	die Adressänderung
computer repair services	der Computer-Reparatur-Service
contents	der Inhalt
country of origin (of the goods)	das Ursprungsland der Waren
customs declaration	die Zollerklärung
customs value	der (Zoll-)Wert
date and signature of sender	das Datum und die Unterschrift des Absenders
declared value - in letters - in numbers	die Wertangabe - in Buchstaben - in Ziffern
destination city, state, country	der Bestimmungsort

district	der Bezirk
document	das Dokument
express-mail service	die Schnellpostsendungen
fee, charge	die Gebühr
for the addressee only	eigenhändig
forward to this address	die Nachsendung an den Empfänger an folgende Adresse
forwarding order	der Nachsendeauftrag
fragile	zerbrechlich
gift	das Geschenk
identification card	der Ausweis
insured letter	der Wertbrief
keyboard	die Tastatur
mail forwarding	der Nachsendeantrag
mailbox	der Briefkasten
main post office	das Hauptpostamt
messenger service	der Botendienst
money order	die Postanweisung
name and address of receiver with indication of the designated country	der Name und die Anschrift des Empfängers mit Angabe des Bestimmungslandes
name and address of sender	der Name und die Anschrift des Absenders
net weight	das Nettogewicht
No unsolicited mail.	Bitte keine Reklame.
non-deliverable	unzustellbar

number of invoices and certificates	die Anzahl der Rechnungen und Bescheinigungen
open/opened	offen/geöffnet
opening hours	die Öffnungszeiten
package	das Paket
parcel/small package	das Päckchen
post office	das Postamt
postage stamp	die Briefmarke
postal charges	die Postgebühren
postal code	der Aufgabeschein
postal form	die Postleitzahl
printer	der Drucker
receipt for official mail	der Rückschein
receipt for registered mail	der Aufgabeschein
registered mail and packages	die eingeschriebenen Briefe und Pakete
return or redirect	bei Rücksendung, die Nachsendung
return to sender	die unverzügliche Rücksendung an den Absender
return to the sender after . . . day(s)	die Rücksendung an den Absender nach . . .Tag(en)
satellite dish	die Satellitenschüssel
sender's instructions in case of non-delivery	Vorverfügungen des Absenders für den Fall der Unzustellbarkeit
signature	die Unterschrift
special notes	besondere Vermerke

stop mail (vacation hold)	das Urlaubspostfach
summary of contents (and number of items in package)	die Inhaltsangabe (und Anzahl der Gegenstände)
tariff calculator	der Tarifrechner
television	das Fernsehen
to be credited to account number . . .	zur Gutschrift auf die Kontonummer . . .
to dispose of freely	als preisgegeben behandeln
to identify yourself	sich ausweisen
to register (letter)	eingeschrieben
urgent	dringend
value	der Wert
zip code	die Postleitzahl

Transportation

Photo Credit: Philippa Tscherkassky

6. TRANSPORTATION

Good to know . . .

The city's website has information in English on driving (rules of the road, getting a driver's license, car sharing and taxi stand); bicycling (traffic rules, route maps, bike rental); parking (short-term parking zones, fees and garages); and public transportation. www.wien.gv.at/english/transportation

Get a good map: *Verkehrslinienplan Wien*, available at subway station ticket offices, shows the whole Vienna public transportation system. Pocket-sized city guides with street indexes are useful to help you navigate the city.

- U-Bahn is underground or subway

- S-Bahn is express train or Schnellbahn

- Strassenbahn is streetcar or tram

Use travel planning websites and tools. Vienna's public transportation (*Wiener Linien*) website, www.wienerlinien.at, provides a detailed guide to the city public transportation system. Smart phone Apps for public transportation include Qando and Wiener Linien, and you can use mobile GPS devices to learn your way around. For biking, the website www.wien.gv.at/verkehr/radfahren provides route maps.

Buy a ticket (*Fahrkarte*) and validate it before you board a bus or train. Stamp your ticket in the blue or orange validation machines (*Entwerter*) inside trams and buses, or at the entrance to U-Bahn or S-Bahn platforms. If you don't have a valid ticket and are stopped by a ticket control agent, the fine is over €100.

Let passengers exit before you enter a bus, tram, U-Bahn or train. If no one gets out, press the red button beside the door or pull the handle sideways to open the door.

Indicate you want to exit when your bus or tram approaches your destination or transfer point, by pressing the "Stop" button next to the exit. Be ready to exit when the vehicle stops.

Don't jaywalk. You can be ticketed for crossing the street against the light or somewhere other than at a crosswalk or corner.

Road signs and parking signs are different around the world. Familiarize yourself with Austria's system.

Maps and Timetables

Here are websites with maps and route information:

- City of Vienna: www.wien.gv.at/stadtplan

- Vienna Transportation Authority
  Wiener Linien: www.wienerlinien.at

- VOR - Vienna Regional Transportation Authority
  Verkehrsnetz Ost-Region: www.vor.at

The VOR and *Wiener Linien* websites offer printable travel planning maps. The address locator displays a map and shows the best walking or public transportation route. You can find fares for travel beyond Vienna's Zone 100 on a zone map on the VOR website.

Train Travel in Austria

Train travel outside of Vienna is convenient. A discounted travel card (*Vorteilskarte*) is available for families and seniors. The Austrian Federal Railways (ÖBB) website is: www.oebb.at/en

Public Transportation

Vienna is famous for its excellent public transportation system. Once you learn your way around, you'll find that it is convenient to get almost anywhere on public transportation.

Within Zone 100, which covers greater Vienna, a regular single ticket, currently €2.10, is valid for all forms of public transportation for 90 minutes in one direction. You can purchase tickets from ticket windows (*Vorverkaufsstellen*) or vending machines (*Automaten*) at U-Bahn stations, or from a tobacconist newsstand (*Tabak-Trafik*). Tickets are not valid until you put a date and time stamp on them when you enter an U-Bahn station, bus or tram.

Children up to age six travel free; children up to age 15 travel free on Sundays, public holidays and Austrian school holidays. You can get a free wallet-sized calendar listing these holidays from most ticket windows. To use this discount, children must have a student ID (*Schülerausweis*).

U-Bahn Information

You can buy maps and timetables, and get free information at these U-Bahn stations:

Erdberg	U3
Floridsdorf	U6
Karlsplatz	U1, U2, U4
Landstrasse	U3, U4

Erdberg	U3
Praterstern	U2
Spittelau	U6
Stephansplatz	U1, U3
Südtiroler Platz/Hauptbahnhof	U1
Westbahnhof	U3, U6

Public Transportation Tickets

You can buy many different public transportation tickets from a ticket window or vending machine at U-Bahn stations, from a bus driver or from a tram ticket machine.

Ticket vending machines (*Automaten*) offer a selection of ticket types, including tickets for bicycles and dogs. Some machines have information and instructions in English. To use a vending machine that accepts cash only, you need coins or €5 or €10 bills. Some vending machines accept bank cards; these have a keypad where you enter your PIN number.

You can order tickets online on the *Wiener Linien* website Ticket Shop.

If you travel beyond Zone 100, buy and validate additional tickets or a multi-zone ticket. You can buy a ticket on a tram or a bus, however it will cost more. Trams have ticket machines in the front car behind the driver, and bus drivers sell tickets for exact change.

Public Transportation Tickets in Vienna

Single-Trip Ticket *Einzelfahrschein*	Valid for a 90-minute single trip within Zone 100. You may change lines, but not interrupt your journey.
Strip Ticket *Streifenkarte*	Each numbered strip on the ticket is valid for a one-hour single trip within Zone 100. You may change lines, but not interrupt your journey. A Strip Ticket costs the same as the equivalent number of Single-Trip Tickets, but offers the convenience of a single paper ticket.
Half-Price Ticket *Halbpreisfahrschein*	For children 6 - 15, dogs and bicycles traveling a single trip within Zone 100. Children under 15 ride free on school holidays.
Senior Ticket *Seniorenfahrschein*	For senior citizens (*Senioren*) over 60. You can purchase these in advance in sets of two. They are valid only in Zone 100.
Short-Distance Ticket *Kurzstreckenkarte*	Valid for rides of one to four stops on trams and buses, or two stops on the U-Bahn and S-Bahn. Boundaries (*Kurzstreckengrenzen*) are announced and shown as black-and-white stripes on route signs.
Vienna Shopping Ticket *Wiener Einkaufskarte*	Valid in Zone 100 for one day from 0800 – 2000. These tickets offer good value for visitors and when you are running errands.

24-hour Vienna Card *24-Stunden Wien Karte*	Valid in Zone 100 for 24 hours from time stamped.
72-hour Vienna Card *72-Stunden Wien Karte*	Valid in Zone 100 for 72 hours from time stamped.
8-Day Card *8-Tage Karte*	A strip ticket valid for unlimited travel within Zone 100 for any eight days, not necessarily consecutive. It is transferable and can be used by multiple riders traveling together.
Weekly Pass *Wochenkarte*	Valid for unlimited travel within Zone 100 for the designated week. A Weekly Pass is transferable; you or your friends or family members can share one pass. While traveling, each person must have his own ticket or pass.
Monthly Pass *Monatskarte*	Valid for unlimited travel within Zone 100 for the designated month. A Monthly Pass is transferable; you or your friends or family members can share one pass. Each person traveling must have a ticket or pass.

Ticket Validation

You must validate your ticket when you board a tram or bus or enter an U-Bahn or S-Bahn station. You stamp a multiple-use ticket for each day of use and for each person using it.

Be sure you fold the ticket and stamp it in numerical order, starting at the number 1. If you cancel out of order, the unused portion of the ticket becomes invalid. If you are caught traveling without a valid ticket, you have to pay a significant fine.

Don't be surprised to see few riders validating tickets. Many public transportation users have yearly or monthly passes.

Ticket Inspection

Plain clothes public transportation agents (*Fahrscheinkontrolle*) regularly check that passengers are traveling with a valid ticket. The fine for traveling without a valid ticket is over €100. If you can't pay the fine but have a photo ID, the agent will give you a bank transfer form. If you don't have a photo ID, you may be taken to the police station to sign a sworn statement. If you don't pay the fine within three days, it will be raised.

Yearly Travel Passes and Special Rates

Discounts are available for yearly pass holders, school children, students and seniors. Go to the Ticket Shop on www.wienerlinien.at to download the appropriate form, and bring it, photo identification, a passport-sized photo and your bank account details to a major U-Bahn station. *Wiener Linien* will send your credit card sized pass in a few weeks. When it's time to renew, you will receive a notice in the mail. To cancel, take your pass and photo ID to a major U-Bahn station one month in advance.

A Yearly Pass (*Jahreskarte*) is valid for one year for unlimited travel within Zone 100. You can use a yearly ticket as a Family Card (*Familienkarte*) on Saturdays from noon to end of service. Two children up to age 15 can travel free in Zone 100 when accompanied by the pass holder. Yearly pass holders may also take a dog or bike for free during specified hours.

Regular yearly passes (*Jahreskarten*) are currently €365 for payment in full. Yearly tickets for seniors (over age 60) (*Jahreskarte für Senioren*) are €224 for payment in full.

Yearly travel tickets for senior citizens are not available from the online ticket shop, as you must provide proof of age to purchase. You may purchase them at the ticket offices (*Vorverkaufstellen*).

Your child may receive an application form from his school for a Student Commuter Pass (*Schülerstreckenkarten*). Complete the form, take it and two photos to the Erdberg Station (U3) School Pass Information counter (*Schülerkartenauskünfte*). This pass allows students to travel between home and school, Monday to Saturday from September to June.

The Afternoon Education Ticket (*Nachmittags-Bildungskarte*) costs extra and allows unlimited travel Monday to Saturday after 1300 and all day Sundays and holidays. When you apply for this pass, bring the student's valid school ID (*Schülerausweis*) and passport-sized photo. You can purchase additional monthly tickets (*Zusatz-Monatskarten*) that allow travel throughout Zone 100 when attached to an existing card.

College and university students can buy reduced fare semester passes (*Semesterkarten*) and monthly passes

(*Hochschüler-Monatskarten*). The *Semesterkarte* is valid from October to January or from March to June. During school vacation months (September, February, July, August, September and February) a student can purchase a Holiday Pass (*Ferien-Monatskarte*). Families who receive government family assistance (*Familienbeihilfe*) are eligible for discounts.

Special discounted travel for students is an excellent deal. The *Top Jugend Ticket* costs €60 and is valid for travel throughout Zone 100 during the school year (September to June).

Smart Phone Tickets and Apps

You can buy online tickets and have tickets digitally displayed on your smartphone. You may also purchase tickets using the *Wiener Linien* Mobile Online Ticketshop using smartphone Apps. You can find these by searching *Wiener Linien* on your mobile device.

Route Planning

Until you are familiar with the routes, you may want to plan your trip before leaving home. Use a transportation map (*Verkehrslinienplan Wien*), a map of the city (*Stadtplan*), or online resources.

To choose the direction of tram, bus, U-Bahn or S-Bahn, you need to know the last stop on the route (*Endstation*). For example, to travel to Vienna International Center from the city center, take the U1 in the direction of Leopoldau.

U-Bahn announcements include door closing, upcoming

stops, and the end of the line. Watch station signs to verify your location: sometimes the announced stops are out-of-sync with the actual stops. New cars have digital signs in each car, showing the next stop and which side of the train to exit. Bus stops are announced, and many buses have a digital display which indicates the next stop. Look for S-Bahn stops on white signs above windows and doors. The conductor announces stops and connecting lines.

U-Bahn routes are color-coded on maps:

| U1 is red |
| U2 is purple |
| U3 is orange |
| U4 is green |
| U6 is brown |

All station signs on each line have the same color.

At tram and bus stops, a *Doppelhaltestelle* sign means the bus stop serves two or more routes.

Most public transportation stops around midnight. Night service on major routes is available from around 0100 until about 0500. On weekends, U-Bahn lines run 24 hours with longer intervals between trains

Special Travel Considerations

During weekends, holidays and evening hours, you may see the word *Kurzzüg* on the digital display above the platform. This means the train will have fewer cars than usual. To board, stand at the designated section of the platform.

On all public transportation, the seats closest to the doors are designated for the disabled, elderly, pregnant women and passengers with babies. Disabled people often wear yellow armbands with black dots. Avoid sitting in a designated seat, or get up when someone who needs it boards.

There are designated areas near the doors for baby carriages and strollers, with straps to hold them in place. Only two baby strollers or two bicycles are allowed per U-Bahn car. If you see one car is occupied, move to the next one. Strollers take precedence over bikes.

Bicycles are allowed on all U-Bahn and S-Bahn lines. Passengers over age 12 may bring a bicycle on board during these hours:

* Monday to Friday 0900 - 1500 and 1830 - end of service
* Saturday 0900 - end of service
* Sunday and holidays all day

Inspectors enforce these hours strictly. If you have a yearly pass, you can take a bike for free; others must purchase a half-price ticket for a bike. You can take your bike on cars marked on the outside with a bicycle symbol. In general, the bicycle entrances are the middle set of doors on U-Bahn cars and the front doors on an S-Bahn. Some S-Bahn cars have special sections where you can strap your bike and sit down. If not, stand with your bike ready to move it to accommodate passengers.

From 0030 - 0500, night buses (*Nachtbuslinien*) run at half-hour intervals on 22 lines. There is a map of the lines on the

Verkehrslinienplan. To see the NightLine schedule online, go to www.wienerlinien.at and click NightLine.

Vienna's public transportation system operates on a different schedule on some holidays. Look for holiday schedule (*Ferientage*) on the signs posted at each stop.

For articles lost and found in public transportation, see the **Safety** chapter.

Travel by Bicycle

Bicycle commuting to work and school, to run errands, deliver packages, transport children and to get to appointments has become increasingly popular in Vienna. Bike lanes are marked on the pavement by a blue circle with a white bicycle in many parts of the city. Do not walk on these lanes; cyclists have the right of way on these paths.

All important traffic junctions and underground stations provide bicycle parking spaces free of charge. As in most cities, bicycle theft is frequent. Buy a good lock and use it, even in your apartment bike storage room. There is an online bike route finder at:
www.wien.gv.at/verkehr/radfahren

Tips for Cyclists

* Wear a helmet!

* Bicycles need a bell, wheel reflectors, and front and back lights.

- Cyclists must obey the same rules of the road as motorists.

CityBike

Bicycles are available for short-term rental at automated rental stations around the city, including many U-Bahn stations, around the Ring, in Stadtpark, at Staatsoper, Schwedenplatz, Stephansplatz and Schwarzenbergplatz. All CityBikes have a basket, lights and a bell. They are fine for short rides on flat surfaces, but not suitable for bike tours. For information on how to register and where to find a bike rental station, see: www.citybikewien.at

To get started, you pay a €1 initial registration fee online or at any rental terminal using a credit card or a bank card. Go to any CityBikeWien station, enter your registration password and select your bicycle by number from the terminal. Adjust the seat, and take a short ride to test the brakes. If you are not satisfied with this bike, try another. Before you leave the rental terminal, identify a return station close to your destination. When you return the bike, ensure that it is firmly locked at the terminal. If the bike is stolen, you will be charged €600 and denied future rentals.

A one-hour rental is free. Longer rentals cost €1 for the second hour, €2 for the third hour, and €4 for the fourth hour and each hour up to a maximum of 120 consecutive hours. If you do not return the bicycle within that time period, CityBikes Wien will automatically charge €600 to your account.

Taxis, Limousines and Car Services

During the day, public transportation is almost always the fastest way to get around. If you are running late, a taxi rarely saves time. Late at night, in bad weather, or if you have mobility problems or heavy packages, a taxi or car service can be more practical.

Taxis

You can find a taxi stand near most major intersections, hotels, U-Bahn and S-Bahn stations, and bus and tram terminals. If a taxi doesn't respond when you hail it, look for a nearby stand.

When calling for a taxi from home, give your district and house address. If you are calling on the street, state the cross streets nearest to you. Specify if you need a station wagon (*Kombiwagen*), a non-smoking taxi (*Nichtraucher*) or if you intend to pay with a credit card (*Kreditkarte*). You may be put on hold while the dispatcher locates a taxi. Try another company if the first one you call can't find a nearby cab. When confirming your order, the dispatcher gives you the number of the taxi and the approximate waiting time.

Taxi fares and extra charges are indicated on the meter. The basic fare is higher at night between 2300 - 0600, and on Sundays and public holidays. There may be an additional charge for luggage. If you go outside the city, the fare may be doubled to pay the driver's way back to a taxi stand.

Limousines and Car Services

Airport Driver and other airport car services offer reliable, less-expensive alternatives to the airport and around town compared to conventional taxis. Car services, unlike taxis, are not on call, do not wait at taxi stands, and cannot be hailed. You must make an appointment, usually several hours or even a day ahead. Call at least 24 hours in advance to reserve transportation to the airport, and earlier during peak travel times or if you need a special vehicle. These services can also be booked online.

- Airport Driver
  +43 1 228 22
  www.airportdriver.at

- C&K Airport Service
  +43 1 444 44
  www.flughafentaxi-wien.at

Taxi Precautions

- For destinations outside Vienna, negotiate the price before you start.

- You can pay by credit card only if the driver accepts your card in advance. Ask before starting you trip.

- You have the right to a complete and detailed receipt (*Quittung*). Ask for it when you get in to the cab. The receipt shows the cab number and company, date, starting point, destination and price.

- If you have a complaint, call +43 1 401 0660. The Vienna Taxi Authority will investigate and, if necessary, submit a report to a disciplinary board.

Driving

Austrian Driver's License

To get an Austrian driver's license (*Führerschein*), go to the HELP website: www.help.gv.at and click on English, then Documents and Identification for details and to download application forms. You will also find driving rules on this website under Free time and Mobility.

The legal driving age in Austria is 18. Austria recognizes EEA and European Union driving licenses. You can convert these to an Austrian license at any time. US citizens and non-EEA residents over age 18 holding a valid national or state driver's license, along with an international driver's license, can drive in Austria for up to six months. After six months, an Austrian driver's license is required.

Apply for a driver's license as soon as you can. The process takes two to three months; you must complete it within six months after you establish residence in Austria. It is illegal to drive without an Austrian driver's license after this time, even if you have applied for an Austrian license.

Exceptions are diplomats and people with diplomatic status who carry an identity card (*Legitimationskarte*) issued by the Austrian Department of Foreign Affairs. Since 1997, the authorities accept a non-Austrian license for diplomats as long as they have a valid license and identification card. However, regulations may change; verify that you have the legal right to drive with your foreign license.

Citizens of many countries, including the US, can have their driver's licenses transferred to Austria (*Führerscheinumschreibung*). This means that you can obtain an Austrian driver's license without having to take a full examination. You can obtain information on driver's license conveyance at the Vienna Transportation Department or at an automobile club.

> Vienna Transportation Department
> *Bundespolizeidirektion Wien Verkehrsamt*
> 9, Josef-Holaubek-Plz. 1
> +43 1 313 100
> www.polizei.gv.at/wien

The office is open for service at 0800, but plan to arrive by 0730 to avoid long lines. Ask at the information window or look for the sign *Austausch ausländischer Führerscheine*.

Bring the following documents:

- original birth certificate (*Geburtsurkunde*)
- original residence registration (*Meldezettel*)
- official photo identification (*amtlicher Lichtbildausweis*) such as a Passport (*Reisepass*) and two copies
- current driver's license and two copies
- two passport-sized photos
- medical report from a doctor on the approved list

- copy of your eyeglass prescription (*Brillenpass*)
- letter or certificate from an optometrist if you wear contact lenses
- €60.50 (subject to change) for the conveyance fee

If you need to take a road test, you will also need:

- original car registration and one copy
- a recent automobile inspection (*Pickerl*) and one copy (unless the car is less than a year old)
- your car registration (*Zulassungsschein*) and one copy
- a letter from your company authorizing you to drive a company car, if you have one

After you submit your application, the authorities will notify you by mail with the details of when and where to take your test. If the authorities determine that you do not need to take a road test, they will notify you by mail when you can collect your license.

Driving School

If the authorities will not transfer your license, you must attend a course at a driving school (*Fahrschule*). Many teachers speak English, and the driving school will help you obtain your license at the end of the course.

Automobile Insurance

All owners of vehicles registered in Austria, as well as temporarily imported vehicles, must have auto insurance (*Autoversicherung*) including third-party or liability insurance

(*Haftpflichtversicherung*). You can arrange for this through an insurance broker (*Versicherungsmakler*) or insurance company. It covers damage caused by your car to other vehicles, persons or property, and financial loss for work missed. If you finance your car, you must have partial or complete comprehensive insurance (*Kaskoversicherung*). Generally, after five or six years, it makes sense to self-insure rather than pay high comprehensive premiums.

Each year, your insurer will send you a form stating that you have international liability insurance. Keep it in your car, along with an accident report form and a pen, in case you are involved in a car accident.

For more about automobile insurance, see the **Banking, Taxes and Insurance** chapter.

Austrian automobile insurance operates on a "Bonus-Malus" basis. A good driving record translates into a discount in premiums and a poor record in higher rates. The discount for a good driving history can be substantial: about 10% per year for each year without a claim, with a maximum benefit of 50%. If you have a good driving record in your home country, ask your insurance carrier for a letter detailing your claims record. Make sure that your insurance agent specifies the number of years since you last had an accident claim in which you were at fault. You can present this to your Austrian insurance agent to request a discount on your premium.

Lost Automobile Documents

You must notify the police if you lose your driver's license, vehicle registration documents or license plates. The police will issue a confirmation that serves as a temporary replacement for the lost documents. If you find a driver's license, vehicle registration document or license plate, take it to the Lost and Found Service Office located at your Municipal District Office.

> Lost Property Hotline
> +43 1 400 0809 1
> www.fundamt.gv.at

Automobile Inspection Sticker

Every car must have an annual automobile inspection. You must display the inspection sticker (*Pickerl*) on the top corner of the passenger side of the windshield. Many auto repair shops conduct the test and issue the sticker. The fee depends on where you take your car and any repairs needed. Keep the letter provided with your sticker; you will need it if the window is replaced or if you sell the car. Auto clubs provide this inspection free for members, or charge about €25 to nonmembers.

Key Driving Facts in Austria

- Every passenger must wear a seatbelt. If you have an accident and are not wearing a seat belt, you will be held at least partially responsible for your injuries.

- Children under age 12 or smaller than 1.5 meters (about 5 ft) are not allowed to sit in the front seat, except in school carpools. Infant car seats in the back seat are mandatory for newborns and babies up to nine months old. The Austrian Automobile Club ÖAMTC rents infant seats.

- Buses and trams always have the right of way. When passing a bus, always signal. You must yield to a bus signaling to leave a bus stop. Be aware of trams: they don't make much noise and can not stop quickly. Tram tracks cross car lanes and the middle of some streets. Cars must stop when a tram is letting passengers off and on.

- Pedestrians about to enter or who have entered a crosswalk have the right of way. You must stop for them.

- Police officers and crossing guards are on duty before and after school hours at crosswalks used by school children.

- Do not block a crosswalk or intersection, or stand over tram lines.

- Unless otherwise indicated, traffic coming from the right has the right-of-way, even in traffic circles. Incorrect driving in and out of traffic circles is a primary cause of accidents involving non-European drivers.

- On narrow streets, cars coming uphill have the right of way over cars traveling downhill.

- You should not honk your horn without a good reason in Vienna.

- You are not permitted to turn right at a red light.

- You are not permitted to turn right without stopping from a one-way street onto a one-way street.

- The red-and-white "lollipop" sign held up by police on the street or in cars means Stop.

- Blue signs with white arrows indicate how you can turn. An arrow pointing left means left only, no right turns; pointing straight, no turns; pointing right, right only, no left turns.

- Drivers must be aware of cyclists.

Highway Sticker

To drive legally on Austrian highways (*Autobahn*), a sticker (*Vignette*) must be visible on the windshield of the car. It is valid for one year, beginning January, and not pro-rated. Gas stations, Tabak-Trafik shops and auto clubs sell them. After a grace period ends in late January, spot checks are frequent and fines are significant. Visitors can purchase short-term stickers that are valid for ten days or two months. There are highways in and around Vienna; you probably need a *Vignette* even if you don't drive outside the city limits.

Traffic Regulations

Failure to adhere to any Austrian traffic regulation (*Verkehrsregel*) can result in a fine, often payable on the spot. Ignorance of the law is no excuse.

When driving, you must have these with you or in your car at all times:

Documents	Safety Equipment
• driver's license • car registration (*Zulassungsschein*) • valid automobile inspection sticker (*Pickerl*) and documentation of inspection • insurance papers, including proof of liability insurance • accident claim form • annual road-tax sticker for highway driving (*Vignette*)	• first aid kit • yellow reflective vest • red warning triangle (*Pannendreieck*) • in winter, snow tires (*Winterreifen*) on your car anywhere in Austria • snow chains (*Schneeketten*) for mountain driving

Here is a summary of Austria's most important driving and traffic laws:

Speed Limits

Unless otherwise indicated, speed limits (*Geschwindigkeitsbeschränkungen*) are:

- 30 km per hour in certain zoned areas
- 50 km per hour within city limits (unless otherwise indicated)
- 100 km per hour on country roads
- 100 km per hour on priority roads with crossroads
- 130 km per hour on highways

A speed limit sign with Zone designates the speed limit for the area, valid until you see another sign with a slash across it.

A white sign with a city name in black letters on the right side of the road designates city limits, which extend until you see the city sign with a red diagonal line through it. If there is a 30 km speed limit sign below the city limit sign, 30 km is the speed limit for the city. Otherwise it is 50 km.

Blood Alcohol Limits

In Austria, you are considered legally drunk if your blood alcohol level is 0.5 parts per thousand or higher. Roadside spot checks are frequent, especially early in the morning and on holidays. Exceeding this limit is punishable by fines of €218 to over €3,600 or possible confiscation of your driver's license.

Cell Phones and Driving

The use of a cell phone while driving is allowed only with a hands-free headset or loudspeaker, unless you are stopped in a traffic jam.

Right of Way

Vehicles coming from the right have the right of way (*Vorrang*). Austrian law and insurance companies will not dispute this, regardless of the apparent fault of a driver to your right in an accident, unless one of these conditions applies:

- steadily moving traffic has priority
- trams and emergency vehicles have the right of way
- the driver to the right forfeits his right of way by clearly indicating so

Traffic Lights

Traffic lights (*Verkehrsampel*) blink five times before changing from green to yellow. During this time, you can enter an intersection. When the light turns yellow, you must stop before the intersection if you can do so safely; if you are already in the intersection, you can proceed through. When the light is yellow, you cannot enter the intersection.

If you are in a lane with an arrow signal, you must turn when the light is green.

Traffic Accidents

If you are involved in a traffic accident, follow these steps:

- stop your car immediately
- put on a yellow reflective vest
- turn on your car's hazard lights
- set up a red warning triangle so traffic behind you can see it
- dial 144 for ambulance, 133 for police if there are injuries or major damage
- establish the circumstances of the accident
- fill out the accident form (*Unfallbericht*) provided by your insurance company
- call your insurance company
- ask for a translation of police reports before you sign

Check with your insurance company before you sign anything. In some instances, you'll need a lawyer to defend your case. You may want to carry legal defense insurance (*Rechtsschutzversicherung*) for this purpose.

On the accident form, exchange this information with the other driver:

- name (including passenger names)
- address
- telephone numbers
- accident details
- make and model of cars
- license plate numbers
- driver's license number (*Führerschein-Nummer*) and place of issue (*ausgestellt von*)
- name of insurance company and policy number on the insurance company form

Automobile Clubs

There are two major automobile associations in Austria. Members receive free roadside assistance and towing. Even if you aren't a member, you can call for help and join on the spot.

ARBÖ
Austrian Auto, Motor and Bicycle League
Auto-, Motor- und Radfahrerbund Österreichs
Call 123 for 24-hour roadside service   www.arboe.at

ÖAMTC
Austrian Automobile, Motorcycle and Touring Club
Österreichischer Automobil-, Motorrad- und Touring Club
Call 120 for 24-hour roadside service   www.oeamtc.at

For an additional yearly fee, members have access to a telephone number for assistance Europe-wide (*Euronotruf*).

Another useful service is an emergency check (*Schutzbrief*), which you can use to pay for roadside service.

Speeding Violations

Police rarely stop drivers for speeding violations. Instead, the authorities issue most tickets when a roadside camera takes a picture of a speeding car. It is possible, but rare, for a civilian or police officer to report you for other violations. If your car is filmed speeding, you will receive a ticket in the mail, often registered, with a bank payment form (*Zahlschein*). You must pay the fine, unless you have compelling evidence to challenge it, even if you have diplomatic status.

Parking

The 1st through 9th, 12th, 14th through 17th and 20th Districts are designated short-term parking zones (*Kurzparkzonen*) where there are time restrictions on parking. Short-term parking is enforced Monday - Friday 0900 to 2200 in some zones, 0900 – 1900 in other zones. The maximum parking duration in all districts is two hours, and in some shopping streets 90 minutes, as indicated on white street signs. An exception is the 15th District where, because of the Stadthalle, parking is restricted September - June 0600 - 2300 daily. You may find other short-term parking zones posted on streets around the city. Hours are listed on signs indicating the start (*Anfang*) and end (*Ende*) of permitted parking. Parking restrictions are strictly enforced between 1800 and 2200.

Parking Vouchers

There are no parking meters in Vienna. Instead, you purchase and display a parking voucher (*Parkschein*) on the dashboard of your car, except on Saturday evening, Sunday and holidays.There are five different vouchers, each one valid for parking up to:

- 15 minutes (free)
- 30 minutes (€1)
- 60 minutes (€2)
- 90 minutes (€3)
- 120 minutes (€4)

You can purchase or pick up parking vouchers at a Tabak-Trafik or auto club. You can place several vouchers on your dashboard, to pay up to the maximum legal parking duration. To fill out your parking voucher:

- mark the month (*Monat*) and day (*Tag*)
- write in the year (*Jahr*)
- mark the current hour (*Stunde*) and next quarter hour, using military time. If you use two or more vouchers, mark the same starting hour on both.

Failure to display a valid parking voucher or pay for parking using cell phone payment is likely to result in a fine.

For posted short-term parking zones outside Vienna, you can use a parking disk, available at a Tabak-Trafik or bank. Set the pointer to the time of your arrival. Cross off the date and time when you park.

Cell Phone Parking Payment

It is possible to pay for parking by SMS (*elektronische Parkgebührensystem* or *Handyparken*). To use this system, first register and pre-pay for parking time on your account. When you park in a short-term parking zone, send an SMS message to a dedicated number, and specify how long you want to park. You will receive an SMS notification when your parking time nears expiration. For more information, see: www.handyparken.at (in German)

Parking Sticker

Residents of the 1st through 9th and the 20th Districts can purchase a yearly parking sticker (*Parkpickerl*) that allows you to park in your district without parking vouchers. You can obtain this sticker from the local district Magistrate Office (*Magistratische Bezirksamt*).You must show your apartment lease, photo ID and automobile documents, including license plate number.

Waiting in Your Car

Usually you can stop your car for up to 15 minutes, but you need to place a 15-minute parking voucher on your dashboard, and mark the time you leave your car, or use *Handyparken*. If you stop on tram rails or in front of a driveway, the driver must remain with the car. Double parking is strictly prohibited. If you stop longer than 15 minutes, the police will fine you.

Towed Cars

The police do not hesitate to have cars towed if they are hindering traffic. If your car is towed, ask at the nearest police station where it has been taken. Most likely, your car is in the impound area south of the city. Every taxi driver knows the way. The registered owner of the car is responsible for paying for the towing and impounding. You must prove ownership by showing the car's registration document and your driver's license. Be prepared to a pay a fine and towing charges of up to €300.

Outdoor Parking Lots

In neighborhoods and small towns, a large blue square sign with the letter P in white indicates public parking lots. There may be an arrow or a distance (in meters) to the actual parking site printed under these signs.

Parking Garages

In the center of Vienna, horizontal lighted signs indicate the name of underground garages and the number of available spaces. Garage parking can be expensive and spaces are tight for large cars. Usually you pay for parking before returning to your car. Most garages are automated; you pay in a payment machine. In many garages you can pay with a bank or credit card as you exit.

You can pick up a free brochure, *Parken in Wien*, from Vienna Tourism for current information. For a map of Vienna showing garages, see: www.wien.gv.at/verkehr/parken/garagen

Shopping Center Parking

Some stores give you a voucher for discounted parking when you make a purchase. The cashier gives you a card that reduces your parking fee.

Park and Ride

Vienna instituted Park-and-Ride to encourage commuters to use public transportation. At locations around the city, drivers can park at an economical rate, and continue their trip on public transportation. www.parkandride.at

Park-and-Ride Locations

U1	• Aderklaaer Strasse
U2	• Donaustadtbrücke
U3	• Erdberg • Ottakring • Hütteldorf
U4	• Heiligenstadt • Spittelau
U6	• Spittelau • Siebenhirten

Car Ownership

Only about one-third of the Viennese own cars; it is expensive to own and operate a car here. In the city center it can be very inconvenient because parking is scarce and ticketing is aggressive.

Car Sharing

Car sharing is popular. CarSharing and Car2Go are two companies providing car-sharing services in Vienna.

For more information see:

- car2go.com/en/wien
- carsharing.at

Garage Space

In many districts, long-term street parking is limited to residents, and costs hundreds of euros per year. Garage spaces are sometimes available in apartment buildings, but are rarely included in the rent. Expect to pay at least €100 per month for space in a parking garage.

New Cars

If you buy a car, expect to pay a 20% VAT tax, insurance premiums, inspection charges and registration fees. If you buy a car here and intend to resell it, German brands and conservative colors sell most easily on the resale market.

Importing a Car

The process of importing a car from outside the EU can be daunting. It is permitted, but the red tape and expense discourage it. Servicing and selling the car may be a challenge especially if it is a brand or model not sold in Austria.

If you are importing a car, you must first get a permission form, then file all forms and get the required inspections within a short time after your arrival in Austria. Your car must meet Austrian environmental standards which can be a costly and time-consuming process. To import a car duty free, you must have driven it for at least six months in your home country.

Used Cars

There are two different categories of car buyers: those who pay Austrian taxes, and those who are tax-exempt because of their diplomatic status. Diplomats, OPEC delegates, IAEA and other UN international staff members often buy a car here and sell it when they leave. This transient population is a good source for low-mileage, recent-model used cars.

ÖAMTC has a fair market valuation service, which provides you with the price for a used car, taking into account mileage and options. This document is useful when you negotiate the price as a seller or a buyer. The purchaser must pay tax on the basis of a government-established value. Some buyers ask the seller to pay this, but there is no obligation to reduce the asking price to include this tax.

Driving with Foreign License Plates

If you import a vehicle, the authorities use your Austrian Residence Registration Service (*Meldebehörde*) to determine if your primary residence (*Hauptwohnsitz*) is in Austria. If not, you may operate the vehicle with foreign license plates for one year from the date you bring the vehicle into Austria. If your primary residence is in Austria, you may drive only with foreign license plates for three days, then you must turn your license plates in to the Austrian Vehicle Registration (*Österreichische Zulassungsbehörde*) where you will be issued an Austrian license plate. Your insurance company can act as your agent.

Requirements vary depending on the vehicle; contact the Technical Inspection Station. Your insurance agent can advise you of the costs.

> Technical Inspection Station
> *Landesfahrzeugprüfstelle*
> 7, Haidequerstr. 5
> +43 1 400 0922 0
> Mon - Fri 0800 - 1200 Thurs 1530 - 1700

Auto Repair

To find a garage for auto repairs, search under *Autoreparatur* plus the type of car plus the district of Vienna where you can take your car. For example, if you live in the 18th District and drive a Volkswagen, the search will be *Autoreparatur Volkswagen 1180 Wien.*

Local Transport Services

If you need to transport a piece of used furniture bought at auction or a load of home improvement materials, you do not have to rent a car. Here are a few options:

Search under *Kleintransporte* or *Botendienste* for delivery services.

Furniture stores such as IKEA and Kika-Leiner, and most home improvement stores, rent vans and trailers by the hour.

Transportation Glossary

End of the short zone	Ende der Kurzstreckenzone
Everyone out, please.	Bitte alle aussteigen.
Please don't speak to the driver.	Bitte nicht mit dem Fahrer sprechen.
Please stand to the right.	Bitte rechts stehen.
The train does not stop (is passing through).	Zug fährt durch.
The train is leaving.	Zug fährt ab.
accident signal	das Pannendreieck
auto insurance	die Autoversicherung
auto repair	die Autoreparatur
automobile	der Personenkraftwagen (PKW)
bicycle	das Fahrrad
bus	der Autobus
city map	der Stadtplan
comprehensive auto insurance	die Kaskoversicherung
driver's license	der Führerschein
driver's license application	der Führerscheinantrag
driver's license conveyance	die Führerscheinumschreibung
driving school	die Fahrschule
express train	die Schnellbahn
ghost driver	der Geisterfahrer
highway	die Autobahn

inspection sticker	das Pickerl
night bus line	die Nachtbuslinie
non-smoking	nichtraucher
official photo ID	der amtliche Lichtbildausweis
parking voucher	der Parkschein
permit parking	das Parkpickerl
receipt	die Quittung
right of way	die Vorfahrt
rules of the road	die Verkehrsregeln
short-term parking zone	die Kurzparkzone
short train	der Kurzzug
short trip boundary	die Kurzstreckengrenze
speed limit	die Geschwindigkeitsbeschränkung
station wagon	der Kombiwagen
student ID	der Schülerausweis
subway	die U-Bahn
ticket sales window	die Vorverkaufsstelle
to buy a ticket	das Ticket kaufen
traffic	der Verkehr
traffic jam	der Stau
traffic light	die Verkehrsampel
train	der Zug
tram	die Strassenbahn
transportation ticket	die Fahrkarte
truck	der Lastwagen (LKW)
validation machine	der Entwerter

Banking, Taxes & Insurance

Photo Credit: Jerry Barton

7. BANKING, TAXES & INSURANCE

Good to know . . .

The euro is the official currency in Austria and many other countries in the European Union. One euro (€) equals 100 euro cents. Coins (*Münzen*) are in denominations of 1 cent, 2 cents, 5 cents, 10 cents, 20 cents, 50 cents, €1 and €2. Bills are in denominations of €5, €10, €20, €50, €100, €200 and €500.

To get euros when you arrive use your ATM card or credit card at an ATM machine (*Bankomat*). You can also change foreign money at a currency exchange agent (*Wechsel*) at airports, train stations or in a bank, but the fee can be a large percentage of the amount you change.

Checks are not used in Austria so you will pay bills, make purchases, and access your money in new ways. Credit cards are accepted at an increasing number of establishments, but many places still only accept cash, an Austrian debit card (*Bankomatkarte*), or credit cards equipped with an embedded chip and PIN.

Open an Austrian bank account and get a debit card (*Bankomatkarte*) to pay at shops and restaurants, access banking services, get account information, and withdraw money from ATM terminals.

Learn Austrian tax regulations by downloading publications in English from the Federal Ministry of Finance website: http://englisch.bmf.gv.at

Get adequate insurance coverage. Austrian insurance agents specialize in health, household, automobile or other types of insurance that are common in Austria, such as legal defense insurance. If you are European, your agents at home may be able to provide insurance for you in Austria. In Austria, insurance agents arrange for the inspection and registration of an imported car, and give you your Austrian license plate.

> *Disclaimer: AWA Vienna offers this information to assist you in setting up financial arrangements, but we are not financial advisors. We recommend that you consult financial professionals in your home country and in Austria for advice suited to your specific situation and needs.*

Austrian Banking

You will need an Austrian bank account (*Bankkonto*) when you live here. When choosing your bank, consider the following:

All large banks in Vienna have English-speaking personal bankers (*Betreuer*). It is important to select a bank where you have a *Betreuer* with whom you can communicate easily. Your *Betreuer* opens accounts, arranges for credit cards and standing orders, and offers advice on the bank's investment services and fees.

Be sure to check for a bank that offers account terms suited to your needs. Ask banks to explain their services and fees. Account maintenance fees (*Kontoführungsprovision*), service charges (*Spesen*), and foreign exchange fees (*Devisenspesen*) vary. These fees may depend on your level of banking activity, amount of money you have in the bank, and types of services you use.

In Austria, if you choose a bank with online banking in English, you can do almost everything online, which means you do not have to go to the bank. Your company will auto-deposit your pay, and you can pay people directly online.

Bank Accounts

As a non-Austrian citizen who lives in Austria, you will be categorized as a foreign resident customer (*Deviseninländer*). Large Austrian banks have a separate department for accounts held by non-Austrian nationals (*Devisenausländer*). Different conditions apply to residents and non-residents, regardless of nationality. Your *Betreuer* can explain and will help you open your account.

There are two major account types: current accounts (*Girokonto*), and savings accounts (*Sparbuch*). Both types are explained in this chapter, but it is very important to open a *Girokonto* so that you can make bank transfers and pay bills.

Most large Austrian banks offer current and savings accounts in major currencies. If you would like a local account in another currency, ask your *Betreuer* about terms and conditions.

To open a bank account you will need:
- your passport
- residence registration (*Meldezettel*)
- employment details if you are employed
- student identification if opening a student account

Depositing cash is the easiest and quickest way to open a new account. You may transfer funds electronically from your foreign bank or open an account with a foreign check, but these options are not recommended due to time delays and fees. Checks are not used in Austria and cashing a foreign check will cost a fee. Depositing a personal check drawn on your overseas bank can take up to several weeks to clear. It is unlikely that you'll be able to cash a personal check in Austria, because banks are reluctant to risk having the check returned due to insufficient funds.

Bank Transfers

As of February 1, 2014, bank transfers (*Überweisung*) within the European Union using the BIC, Bank Identifier Code (SWIFT) and the International Bank Account Number (IBAN) will take no more than 24 hours during the week. Whether domestic or foreign, a bank-to-bank transfer can be overnight. If you are transferring funds outside the EU, and you are transferring funds between member banks of the Society for Worldwide Interbank Financial Telecommunications (SWIFT), the typical transfer time is three to four working days. To expedite the process, ask your home bank for the best way to communicate transfer instructions. When transferring or depositing foreign currency, the rate of exchange (*Devisenkurs*) can vary among banks. The foreign exchange fee (*Devisenspesen*) and other bank charges may depend on the amount of money you have in the bank and the kinds of services you use. Ask about rates and fees before you initiate a transfer.

Current Accounts

An Austrian current account (*Girokonto*) is your main source of readily-available cash. Most people use their *Girokonto* to make fund transfers to pay for goods and services, as well as rent, utilities, and other routine recurring costs. See "Payment Methods" in this chapter for a description of procedures to follow when you make these payments.

Overdraft Protection

You earn very little interest on balances in a current account, but you can arrange for an overdraft limit (*Überziehungsrahmen*), the convenient equivalent of a small loan or cash advance. The bank will charge interest on the overdrawn balance, but usually much less than the interest on the equivalent unpaid balance on a credit card. Overdraft limits and interest charges vary, so ask your bank. In general, banks will settle all account charges including overdraft interest by debiting your account quarterly. Details of the charges will appear on your account statements.

Debit Cards

Every *Girokonto* comes with a debit card (*Bankomatkarte*) connected to the account that:

* serves as your bank ID when you visit your bank

* gains entry into your bank's lobby where special machines are located that enable you to access self-service banking transactions, including after hours in most cases; in larger banks, the lobby is available 7 days a week, 24 hours a day

* enables you to get cash from ATM terminals all over Austria and much of the world

* enables you to pay at grocery stores, most shops and some restaurants

* functions as a "paypass" card for transactions under €25

To pay with a bank card after the cashier, salesman, or waiter has entered the transaction details:

- insert your card into the machine, positioning the magnetic strip as indicated
- enter your PIN code
- confirm the amount of the payment by pressing the green *Bestätigung* button
- take your receipt and your card

Your bank then debits your account automatically. Most banks restrict Bankomat payments to €1,100 weekly, in addition to the daily limit of €400 for cash withdrawals. Shops like the Bankomat system because they pay a smaller fee for transactions and you pay nothing at all.

To withdraw cash from a bank machine:

- insert your card
- choose your language if possible
- enter your PIN code when prompted
- enter the amount you want to withdraw
- press the green *Bestätigung* button to confirm the amount
- withdraw your money and your card

If you want to cancel a step or change a number you entered, press the yellow correction button (*Korrektur*). To cancel the transaction, press the red cancel button (*Abbruch*). If you enter your PIN code incorrectly, you can re-enter it twice. If you enter it incorrectly a third time, the machine will cancel your transaction and keep your card. If this happens, contact the bank where the machine is located. If you forget your PIN code, notify your bank, and they will give you a new code.

There is no charge for withdrawing money from any bank in the Euro zone.

Most banks permit you to withdraw daily up to €400 (or its equivalent in other currencies). If you need to withdraw more than that, you can do so in cash (*Barauszahlung*) at the bank's cashier window (*Kassa*) during regular business hours, or at the indoor machine (*Geldausgabeautomat*) where you can withdraw €1,500 daily at most banks. Amounts may vary, so check with your bank.

You might find a red sign near where you insert your card. This means the machine is out of order (*ausser Betrieb*). Usually there is a list posted next to the machine with the locations of other nearby Bankomat. A green sign means the machine is working (*in Betrieb*).

Savings Accounts

A savings account (*Sparkonto*) earns interest, although the amount varies by bank. As in most countries, a simple savings account earns the lowest interest rate, but has no restriction on how long you must leave your funds in the account. Fixed deposits range from six months to six years, and earn higher interest rates. They have different names at different banks, like *Vermögenssparbuch* and *Kapitalsparbuch*. You can withdraw funds before the term expires, but you will forfeit most of the interest earned. Ask about conditions before committing your money.

Local banks deduct tax on interest earned on your accounts. In addition, dividends earned on Austrian bank accounts are subject to withholding tax. Currently, the tax authorities receive a flat rate of 25% of capital income. For Austrian residents, this tax has already been paid, so you do not need to state this income on your Austrian tax return. If you are not a resident of Austria or the EU, and you prove your status (*Devisenausländerschaft*) at your bank, your interest is not subject to the withholding tax. Your withholding tax on dividends may be reduced, depending on the tax treaty between your home country and Austria. However, you must declare this income when you file your taxes in your country of residence. If you declare yourself a member of a diplomatic mission or a non-Austrian resident, you will not qualify for certain government subsidies.

Bank Charges

Ask about the service fees (*Kontoführungsgebühr*) that are applied to your account. Each quarter you will be charged:

- a fee for the bank account itself (*Kontoführungsprovision*)
- a fee for each transaction (*Umsatzprovision*)
- a credit for interest on the account balance accrued that quarter (*Habenzinsen*)
- tax on the interest accrued that quarter (*Kapitaletragsteuer*)

Since you pay tax on your account interest through your bank, you do not need to declare it on your Austrian taxes, however it may affect your home country tax declaration.

Payment Methods

The fees a bank charges for establishing payments depend on the type of account you have. In general, most banks include these charges in your monthly account fees, but charge a nominal amount for each change or cancellation. Your bank is responsible for executing accurate, on-time payments. Mistakes are rare. However, if you discover a delayed or incorrect payment, or a payment in error, notify your bank immediately.

Your banker will help you set up payment methods.

Account-to-Account Transfers

The most common method of payment in Austria is a bank transfer (*Überweisung*) from a current account (*Girokonto*). You make a bank transfer to pay a bill (*Rechnung*) from your current account. If you want to use funds in a savings account to pay a bill, you first transfer the money to a current account, then make the payment.

Payment Orders

One Time Payments: if you prefer, you can take a payment order form and cash to a bank to make a payment. If you don't have an account at that bank, you must pay a fee to have the payment processed.

Recurring Payments: you can pay recurring bills with payment orders. Many people pay bills for rent, gas, electricity, telephone service, radio and television fees, insurance premiums, tuition, and credit card balances with standing orders. There are two types of orders that you can establish with your bank to make recurring payments:

- Fixed Standing Order (*Dauerauftrag*) pays the same amount every month on the same day. You can set this up yourself online, or your *Betreuer* can help you.

- Direct Debit Payment Order (*Einziehungsauftrag*) allows a company to deduct a fixed amount from your account, for example, your landlord books your monthly rent payment. The other form of direct debit payment order (*Abbuchungsauftrag*) authorizes the bank to pay a bill in full, regardless of the amount. Internet, phone, and electric bills must be paid with this kind of order. The payee of a direct debit payment order must send you advance notification by email or post of the amount and date of the upcoming payment. This allows you to deposit money into your account or to question the amount of a bill. You can change or cancel a standing payment order at any time.

- Sweep Order (*Abschöpfungsauftrag*) allows you to establish a maximum balance in an account, and when that balance is exceeded, the overage is automatically transferred to another account.

Transfer and Payment Forms

Transfer forms (*Erlagschein*) and payment order forms (*Zahlschein*) are available at your bank. These forms may be preprinted with the your bank's name and BIC, or blank for you to fill in. Using your IBAN and BIC, with your name and reason for payment clearly printed on your transaction form, your payment will be received quickly, and the bank will have ample proof of your transaction. Domestic transfers within Austria only need the IBAN.

When you owe money, you may be given an *Erlagschein* form with the company's name, BIC and IBAN. Or you may receive a bill for services (*Honorarnote*), from a doctor, for example. Many businesses, especially medical and legal professionals, include their IBAN and BIC on their letterhead, and submit their bills in the form of a letter stating the amount due. When you complete a payment form, make sure to clearly print your name and the reference or invoice number. Otherwise, the recipient may not be able to identify the source of the payment.

You can use a machine at your bank to make payments with payment forms. You receive a stamped receipt as proof of the payment. You can also see the transaction in online banking and print out a confirmation, if needed.

Here are some helpful terms for filling out your bank's forms:

* *Empfängerin* – recipient (payment recipient must give you their account name)

* *IBAN Empfängerin* – IBAN of the recipient account

* *BIC Empfängerin* – BIC of the recipient account

* *Betrag* – the amount you wish to transfer (Note: some banks use a decimal point to indicate cents, some use a comma)

- *Verwendungszweck* – the purpose of the transfer, such as your billing reference number or invoice number (*Rechnungsnummer*)

- *Kontoinhaberin/Auftraggeberin* – account holder: Sign your name

- *Kontoinhaberin/Auftraggeberin* – IBAN and BIC for your account from which the money is being transferred

Austrians take their privacy seriously, and so do their banks. If you do not complete the forms clearly and completely, your transaction may not go through, or the payee may not be able to identify that the payment came from you. Your bank is not allowed to tell them. It's the law.

Online Banking

Online banking is very popular in Austria, because it is easy, convenient and secure. Ask your bank representative for details on how your bank's system works. Most pages of most online banking sites are available in English. Many banks allow you to print your bank statement online, and you can view your transactions and banking activity online.

A user name and password will be issued to you by your bank so you can access your account anytime using any computer with an internet connection. With online banking, you will receive a TAN code to confirm most online transactions, such as paying bills, setting up automatic payments, and changing details of those payments. When you are asked to sign (*Unterschrift*) your online transaction, a TAN code is sent to your cell phone by SMS. It is valid for two minutes only.This system is very secure.

Credit Cards

An Austrian credit card (*Kreditkarte*) has a few unique features. The credit limit on your credit card will depend on your relationship with your bank and your income. Your monthly balance will be automatically withdrawn from your current account. If your credit card is lost or stolen and you report it to the credit card company within 24 hours, you are not liable for misuse of the card. If you report it after 24 hours, your liability is limited.

Bank Services

There are two types of counters at your bank:

* the cashier window (*Kassa*) where money changes hands

* the transaction counter, where banks conduct business not involving cash - this is where you order new bankcards and PIN codes, resolve problems or get help operating a machine

Safe Deposit Boxes

You can rent a safe deposit box (*Safe*) at most banks. A safe deposit box must be rented in the name of a person. Rental rates vary by the size of the box. You will receive a key and a code. Some banks use fingerprint readers. Your *Betreuer* will show you how to access your *Safe*.

Bank Statements

For a service charge, your bank may mail your account statements (*Kontoauszug*) to you. You can also ask your bank to hold your statement and transaction notices (*Belege*) at the bank. However, most people print their own statements online or at a bank branch.

Self-Service Kiosks

Along with the standard ATM and the payment machine that accepts payment forms (*Erlagschein*), most banks have an Account Statement (*Kontoauszug*) machine which allows you to:

- check your account balance

- print your monthly statement for free. Insert your Bankomat card as pictured on the machine, and follow the instructions. The machine will print details of all transactions since you last made a request, and show your starting and ending balances.

Your personal banker or another bank employee will show you how each of the machines work.

Banking Hours

Monday to Friday 0800 – 1230, 1330 – 1500
Thursday 0800 – 1230, 1330 – 1730
Saturday, Sunday and holidays closed

The headquarters (*Zentrale*) of major banks usually do not close for lunch.

How to Pronounce Numbers in German

In German, numbers between 20 and 99 are in the reverse order of the way your write them. For example, you write 21 in German, but you say "one-and-twenty" (*einundzwanzig*). To help you understand numbers, try writing them as you listen, and leave a space for the tens digit. When you hear 142, (*einhundertzweiundvierzig*) "one hundred two and forty," write "1" for "*einhundert*," leave a space, then write "2" for "*zwei*," then write "4" between the two digits for "*undvierzig*." If you are confused or uncertain about an amount, a price, or a number, ask the person to write it down or repeat it slowly, "*Langsamer, bitte.*"

Tax Regulations

You can download a variety of publications on Austrian tax regulations in English from the website of the Federal Ministry of Finance (*Bundesministerium für Finanzen*): http://englisch.bmf.gv.at

Individual Income Tax

Residents of Austria are liable for income tax (*Einkommensteuer*) on their worldwide income and on some types of capital gains. You are considered a resident if you spend more than six consecutive months in Austria or have a dwelling in Austria. Nationals of European Union countries are treated as residents for tax purposes if 90% of their income comes from Austria, or if their non-Austrian income is below a certain amount. Austria taxes a husband and wife separately, and a child separately from his parents. In general, to calculate your taxable income, deduct allowable business and personal expenses from your net income. Allowable expenses include social security premiums, special personal expenses and extraordinary charges. For more information, consult a tax advisor.

For US Citizens

If you are an American citizen who earned income in the US, you must file a yearly tax declaration with the IRS. New laws make specific requirements of you. Living abroad does not suspend your tax filing obligations to the IRS in any way, and in fact increases your responsibilities in filing reports on your foreign bank accounts. You can get up-to-date information from the Association of American Residents Overseas (AARO) and American Citizens Abroad (ACA) websites. Your accountant can help you make the necessary filings.

Expatriate Relief

Up to 35% of an expatriate employee's taxable income may be tax-free if it qualifies as reimbursement of certain expenses. These expenses qualify if your employer reimburses them:

- moving expenses
- double household costs
- school costs for your children
- travel expenses to a foreign headquarters or residence

There are limits on the amount of individual expenses that you can deduct. Ask your employer and your tax advisor if you qualify.

Diplomatic Status Taxation

Members of diplomatic missions in Austria, their families and their household employees are not liable for Austrian income tax if they are not Austrian citizens or permanent residents of Austria. However, if they earn income from Austrian sources, they must pay tax on it as non-resident income.

Value-added Tax

The standard value-added tax VAT (*Mehrwertsteuer* or *MwSt*) is 20%. However, Austria imposes a 10% VAT on rent paid for apartments and homes, and on food, farm products, and other essentials. Members of diplomatic missions in Austria may buy goods and services free of Austrian VAT as long as they do not have Austrian citizenship or permanent residency in Austria.

Automobile Tax

Austria imposes a special automobile tax (*Normverbrauchsabgabe* or *NOVA*) on all car purchases. To calculate the NOVA, multiply the net value of the automobile (excluding VAT) by a percentage based on fuel consumption. Then, add the standard VAT on the net value of the car plus the NOVA.

See www.nova-reher.at/index.php/rechner-menu/mvst2014 for an online calculation (German).

Real Estate Tax

Owners of Austrian real estate must pay an annual municipal real estate tax (*Grundsteuer*) ranging from 0.8% to 1% of the property's tax value, that is considerably below market value. Transfers of real estate are generally subject to a 3.5% tax (*Grunderwerbsteuer*) on the sale price or market value. In addition, a 1% registration fee is payable on the sale of real estate.

Insurance

Your insurance (*Versicherung*) needs depend on your circumstances. Compulsory insurance, standard contracts, and services vary from country to country. Assess the value of your property and define your health coverage requirements. Research and compare terms, costs and policies to ensure that the compensation you may receive covers your medical expenses, property damage, or loss. Adequate insurance gives you peace of mind and is vital to your safe and healthy stay abroad.

Look for insurance agents who speak English or your native language, have experience with foreigners, and understand that insurance differs greatly from one country to another. You may need to find multiple agents to adequately address all of your insurance needs. Different agents specialize in providing health, household, automobile, or other types of insurance that you may not be familiar with, but that are common in Austria, such as legal defense insurance. If you are European, your agents at home may be able to provide insurance for you in Austria. For information on health insurance, see "Medical Insurance" in **Health Care**.

Household Insurance

You need to arrange for household insurance before your goods arrive at your new home, so be prepared with an inventory and an estimate of the value of major items and valuables when you speak to an agent. Carry copies of receipts, appraisals and photographs separately from your shipment. Depending on the kind of coverage you have in your home country, your insurance may become invalid when you leave your home or when your household effects leave the moving van. Check the conditions of your policy to make sure your belongings remain covered continuously.

Check the details and the length of your insurance policy before you sign; some agents specify a long commitment that makes it difficult for you to change agents or companies if you are not satisfied.

Jewelry and valuables coverage is limited in standard insurance policies. You cannot attach a rider to your policy unless you have a very heavy or built-in safe in your home to store your valuables. Because burglaries are a growing problem in Vienna, you may want to consider buying a safe, or leaving your valuables in a bank safety deposit box.

Basic household insurance covers risks such as fire, explosion, lightning, theft and vandalism, and damage as a result of water, steam and rain. Tenants are legally liable for damage to rented property, and must carry renter's insurance.

Some policies cover your belongings on the basis of replacement value, others on the basis of market value. Most Austrian insurance policies indemnify on the basis of new value. You should value your belongings accurately; keep receipts, appraisals and photographs to document important items. If the real value of your belongings exceeds the insured value, you will be underinsured in the case of loss.

Automobile Insurance

In Austria, an insurance agent arranges for the inspection and registration of an imported car, and also gives you your license plate. Motor vehicle registration is complicated, and clerks prefer to deal with agents who do this routinely. You need to transfer your car's registration shortly after arriving in Austria. You need an Austrian license plate to get a district parking sticker in Vienna.

If you have original documents for your car and proof of a good driving record, you can benefit from reduced premiums for accident-free driving. This is called the *Bonus-Malus* system. You can have your insurance premiums reduced by up to 50%.

You must have liability insurance. If you finance your car, you must also have comprehensive coverage (*Vollkasko*).

Travel Insurance

The two kinds of travel insurance (*Reiseversicherung*) are personal loss and medical expenses.

Personal loss travel insurance protects you if your money is lost or stolen while traveling, or if you must cancel a trip for health reasons. It also covers you against theft and lost luggage. Often you can purchase a one-time travel insurance policy with your tour package or flight ticket. If you travel frequently, continuous travel insurance can be a good choice.

The second type of travel insurance covers medical emergencies away from home. Many medical insurance policies for expatriates make it unnecessary to take out other travel insurance policies if you stay within a specified geographic region. If you travel outside the area of coverage, you need an additional travel insurance policy.

Personal Liability

Liability insurance (*Haftpflichtversicherung*) provides you with coverage for injury or damage you cause to others or to their property. This is true of automobile as well as household liability insurance.

Personal accident insurance (*Unfallversicherung*) indemnifies you from financial consequences of a serious accident. This type of policy will pay a lump sum in case of permanent disability or death, thus reducing the financial loss for the insured or the surviving relatives.

Many Austrians have legal defense insurance (*Rechtsschutzversicherung*) to cover the expenses of legal advice or representation. If you buy a legal defense policy, choose one that allows you to hire your own lawyer. This insurance may be beneficial because Austrians firms are quick to engage a law firm in even minor disputes, and differences between tenants and landlords or real estate management firms are frequent, especially at the end of a lease.

Pet Insurance

There are two ways you can insure your pets: through a pet health insurance policy or through your household liability insurance policy.

Pet health insurance (*Haustierversicherung*) rates and coverage vary by the type of pet and coverage. If you live in an apartment, you need liability insurance in case your pet bites someone or damages someone else's property.

Banking, Taxes and Insurance Glossary

accident insurance for serious injury	die Unfallversicherung
account maintenance fee	die Kontoführungsprovision
account number	die Kontonummer
account statement	der Kontoauszug
amount	der Betrag
ATM card	die Bankomatkarte
Automatic Teller Machine (ATM)	der Bankomat
bank sorting code	die Bankleitzahl (BLZ)
bank transfer	die Überweisung
bearer	der Überbringer
bill	die Rechnung
booked entry	die Buchung
cash	das Bargeld, Bar
cash deposit	die Bareinlage
cash withdrawal	die Barabhebung
cashier	die Kassa
claim	der Anspruch
coins	die Münzen
comprehensive auto insurance	die Vollkaskoversicherung
confirmation	die Bestätigung
credit cards	die Kreditkarten
currency	die Währung

current account	das Girokonto
deductible	der Selbstbehalt
exchange rate	der Devisenkurs
fees	die Spesen
fixed standing payment order	der Dauerauftrag
foreign currency exchange	die Wechselstube
foreign customer (non-resident)	der Devisenausländer
foreign exchange rate	der Devisenkurs
foreign resident customer	der Deviseninländer
health insurance	die Krankenversicherung
household insurance	die Haushaltsversicherung
insurance	die Versicherung
insurance agent	der Versicherungsberater
insurance policy	die Versicherungspolizze
invoice (for goods)	die Rechnung
invoice (for professional services)	die Honorarnote
legal defense insurance	die Rechtschutzversicherung
liability insurance (required)	die Haftpflichtversicherung
machine to print account statements	der Kontoauszugsdrucker
merit-rating insurance system	das Bonus-Malus-System
paper money	die Scheine
password	das Passwort

person authorizing a payment	der Auftraggeber
pet insurance	die Haustierversicherung
premium	die Prämie
preprinted transfer form	der Zahlschein
reason for payment	der Verwendungszweck
recipient of a payment	der Empfänger
receipt	die Quittung
receipt (for a transaction)	der Beleg
safe-deposit box	die Safe
savings account	das Sparbuch
savings book	das Sparbuch
securities	die Wertpapiere
self-service banking center	die Selbstbedienung (SB)
to transfer	überweisen
travel insurance	die Reiseversicherung
variable standing payment order	der Abbuchungsauftrag, der Einziehungsauftrag

CHILDREN

Photo Credit: Wendy Williams

8. CHILDREN

Good to know . . .

The Vienna Babies Club is a great way to make friends and access information and resources for mothers of toddlers and mothers-to-be. See www.viennababiesclub.at

Expectant mothers need a Mother-Child Passport to receive child benefits and must register with a hospital for the birth. Familiarize yourself with financial support options for expecting and new parents. Within the first week after birth, a child requires a birth certificate, residence permit and registration and eventually a passport.

Vienna is full of fun activities for kids including playgrounds, a world-class zoo, special children's museums, and the Prater – a huge amusement and sports complex.

Top Five Fun Places for Kids

1. Playgrounds around every corner: try Rathaus Playground at Rathausplatz in the 1st District
2. Prater: walk past the amusement park to get to the "green" Prater with playgrounds, a kids train, and sports facilities of every kind
3. Schönbrunn Zoo: Europe's best and oldest zoo
4. Swimming pools, beaches and water playgrounds: try the Danube Island Water Playground
5. Haus des Meeres: aquarium and terra park built into an old anti-aircraft tower

New Mothers

Welcoming a new child is a wonderful, if hectic, experience that can feel even more overwhelming in a new country. Familiarize yourself with the paperwork that should be filed after birth so that you are prepared. Government assistance is available to most parents; knowing the details of the paperwork required can help avoid some headaches.

Maternity leave policies in Austria may be different from those in your home country. It is usually in your best interest to inform your employer early about a pregnancy. There may be specific working restrictions and legal protection. Most working Austrian mothers will begin maternity leave eight weeks prior to their due date and return to work in some capacity anywhere from 12 to 24 months after birth.

Registration for Child Benefits

If you are one of the 17,000 people in Vienna with diplomatic status and you did not complete a residence registration form (Meldezettel), you may have some difficulty, as the form is required for almost every government transaction outlined in this chapter. Generally, your Legitimation Card will work as a substitute, however, without a Meldezettel, you will need to apply on paper and possibly in person instead of using online registration systems.

The child care subsidy is available to families with diplomatic status. Maternity pay appears to be done on a case-by-case basis and may be worth applying for if you are not sure of your eligibility.

Birth Registration

Before your baby arrives, begin the process of getting the relevant forms and stamps.

Mother-Child Passport (*Mutter-Kind Pass*)
Your obstetrician will provide you with a *Mutter-Kind Pass*, a booklet to track your pre-natal check-ups, your child's immunizations, and regular check-ups through the first years. Initially, your doctor and then your child's pediatrician will stamp and sign pages which you will need to qualify for benefits, like the baby package (*Wäschepaket*) and maternity benefits (*Kinderbetreuungsgeld*).

Diaper Backpack (*Wickelrücksack*)

Any child born in Vienna, regardless of your insurance plan, can receive a Diaper Backpack from the city that includes free samples of diapers and creams, a variety of literature on Vienna's services for children and families, plus a thick book of coupons. To receive your present, take your Mutter-Kind-Pass to your local Parent-Child Center (*Eltern Kind Zentrum*) as soon as eight weeks before your due date.

Birth Certificate (*Gerburtsurkunde*)

After your baby is born, your first step will be to get a birth certificate (*Geburtsurkunde*). The hospital fills out a pre-registration form and sends it to the Registrar of Births (*Standesamt*) for the district (*Bezirk*) where your baby was born (not the district where you live). The hospital gives you a card to take to the Registrar of Births. Some hospitals have a Registrar on site, which saves you a trip to the office. Your baby must be registered within one week of birth, but it usually takes several days for the hospital's form to be received by the Registrar.

To register your baby, you need the following documents if you and the father are married:

- parents' birth certificates
- marriage certificate of parents
- proof of parents' nationality
- parents' *Meldezettel*

If the you and the father are not married, the father needs to come in person to register and you need:

- mother's birth certificate
- mother's proof of nationality
- mother's *Meldezettel*
- acknowledgement of paternity
- father's proof of nationality
- father's *Meldezettel*

Check the spelling of all names carefully; all future documents are based on this form. You can request additional copies of the birth certificate. Your child receives two birth certificates: an Austrian one and an international one (*Auszug aus dem Geburtseintrag*) in ten languages.

A baby born in Austria is *not* automatically entitled to Austrian citizenship.

Registration and Austrian Residence Permit

Apply for your baby's registration (*Meldezettel*) at your Municipal District Office (*Magistratische Bezirksamt*) as soon as possible after the birth, at the latest within three days of returning home from the hospital. If the *Meldezettel* is completed in the hospital, it may be possible to collect the *Meldezettel* at the same time as the *Geburtsurkunde*. Take the following documents with you:

- child's Austrian birth certificate
- official photo ID of the person registering the child
- *Meldezettel* filled out for the child

For a child to obtain an Austrian residence permit (*Aufenthaltsbewilligung*), you need these documents:

- parents' *Meldezettel*
- passports of the child and both parents
- child's Austrian birth certificate

Maternity Pay and Financial Assistance

If you live in and are registered in Vienna, you are eligible for some level of child assistance. These programs are administered separately and have different eligibility requirements. Options vary depending on your circumstances, but the support offered is definitely worth investigating.

Maternity Pay

Maternity leave and benefits vary by occupation. If you work in Austria as a professional office employee, maternity pay benefits begin a minimum of eight weeks before your anticipated due date and eight weeks after the birth, or 12 weeks post-birth for a caesarean section. You can apply for maternity benefits either before or after the birth of your child at the local office of the health insurance (*Gebietskrankenkasse Bezirksstelle*).

Family Assistance (*Familienbeihilfe*)

Regardless of working status during pregnancy, mothers and fathers are eligible for a monthly child benefit provided that at least one parent has social health insurance in Austria. Family assistance (*Familienbeihilfe*) is based on the age of the child and the number of children in the household. Apply at your district's tax office (*Finanzamt*).

Maternity Benefits

If your family receives family assistance, you are also eligible for maternity benefit payments (*Kinderbetreuungsgeld*). You can choose between several benefit options that vary in length of time. Payments are dependent on getting necessary check-ups and signatures in the Mother-Child Passport.

Family Support Service

The city's Youth and Family Welfare Office (MA11) offers a variety of services for children and families. Local district offices register you for your Diaper Backpack and offer weight checks for your newborn, assistance relating to child support, counseling, conflict management, crisis intervention and much more.

Austrian Youth and Family Welfare Office (MA11)
Amt für Jugend und Familie
www.wien.gv.at/menschen/magelf

Childcare, Kindergartens and Playgroups

Infants and toddlers and their mothers have many options for childcare. In-home daycare, nannies and babysitters, *au pairs*, and even rent-a-granny are all available in addition to larger childcare centers. Childcare in Vienna underwent major changes in 2009 when private daycare became subsidized and more places became available. Parents pay only €60-250 per month to cover food, additional help and activities. It is now common to find one and two year olds in daycare centers, although some families still wait until age three.

In Austria, the general term *Kindergarten* encompasses all daycare or pre-school settings prior to the beginning of elementary or primary school (*Volksschule*) at age six or seven. Most Kindergartens divide children by age, with a younger group from roughly ages one to three and an older group from three to six.

Childcare Options

- In-home daycare for newborn to 5 years (*Tagesmutter,Tagesvater*)

- Babysitter/Nanny for newborn to 5 years

- Rent-a-Granny (*Leih-Oma*)

- *Au Pair*

- Daycare for age 1 to 3 (*Kleinkindergruppe, Kinderkrippe*)

- Parent-run nursery school for age 3 to 6 (*Kindergruppe*)

- Daycare for age 3 to 5 (*Kindergarten*)

- Mandatory Kindergarten for age 6 (*Kinderhort*)

Finding a Caregiver or Kindergarten

Babysitters

Ask for recommendations from friends, through the AWA, Vienna Babies Club classifieds or at the international schools.

Au Pairs

Under Austrian law, the host family of an *au pair* must submit a formal notification of employment in advance to the Public Employment Service of Austria (*Arbeitsmarktservice* or *AMS*). You can arrange this through an authorized *au pair* agency (a current listing is maintained by the Vienna Babies Club). If you make private arrangements, you can find information and forms on the AMS website: www.ams.at/english

In-home Nurseries, Nannies and Private Kindergartens

Ask for recommendations in your neighborhood or see: www.kinderdrehscheibe.at

Public Kindergartens

Ask at the Kindergarten Service office (MA-10) or check online at: www.wien.gv.at/bildung/kindergarten/kdg/

Kindergarten Registration

Generally you must first register with the Kindergarten office for a customer number before getting on a waiting list. If possible, register in January or February to start in September. If you have residency you can apply online, while those with diplomatic or other statuses are still eligible but will need to apply in person at the Kindergarten Service Center (MA10) for your district.

Important Links

Registration Information:
www.wien.gv.at/bildung/kindergarten/anmeldung

Find your service center:
www.wien.gv.at/bildung/kindergarten/servicestellen

For more information on schooling for all ages, see the chapter *Education*.

Playgroups

The Vienna Babies Club (VBC) offers playgroups based on the age of your child, as well as district-based groups and hobby and social groups. Check out:
www.viennababiesclub.com

Some churches offer English-language community and playgroups. Check the bulletin boards at your local Parent-Child Center, church, or supermarket for groups. Most will be German-speaking, but a majority of young Austrians speak at least some English.

Parents' Legal Responsibilities

In Austria, parents are legally liable if their child suffers a serious injury or illness, such as a bicycle accident or poisoning, while under their supervision. In such events, the examining doctor is required to report the incident to the appropriate authorities, who will investigate.

Car Seat Laws

Car seats are required for children up to age 12 and 1.5 meters tall. Newborns and babies up to nine months or nine kilos must sit in a rear-facing infant car seat, and never in a seat with an airbag. You can buy car seats in department stores or drugstores, or rent car seats from the ÖAMTC.

Children up to 18 kilos must sit in a booster seat. Austrian law also requires children under 12 to sit in the back seat. Children age 12 and older, or at least 1.5 meters tall, may sit in the front seat with a seatbelt. If you are a member of ÖAMTC, you can take your car and car seat to a local office for a free seat safety inspection. For more information see *Driving* in the **Transportation** chapter.

Shopping

Everything you and your child need — new and used kids clothes, furniture, strollers, cribs — is readily available. The Vienna Babies Club and international schools have semi-annual flea markets where you can find bargains. Vienna is filled with boutique stores for children and all major department stores have large children's sections.

Nursery Furniture

You can find used children's furniture at flea markets at the international schools in Vienna. The Vienna Babies Club is another source for quality used children's and baby clothing, maternity wear, furniture and accessories. The Vienna Babies Club's members-only notice board allows members to post items for sale or announce items required. American Women's Association members can post on the Facebook Group.

If you are bringing a crib from another country, make sure you bring bedding as well.

Bed Sizes

US Crib	52" x 27 ½"	132 cm x 70 cm
European Crib	47¼" x 23.6"	120 cm x 60 cm
European Junior Bed	63" x 27 1/2"	140-160 cm x 70 cm
European Kids bed	78 ¾" x 35.4"	200 cm x 90 cm
US Twin bed	75" x 39"	190½ cm x 99 cm

Baby Formula, Food and Diapers

- Breast feeding is encouraged and openly practiced.

- Baby formula is available in powdered form. It is safe to add Viennese tap water. Special formulas are available, including soy-based and allergy free products. Ask your doctor for details.

- You can find a variety of jarred baby food, fruit pouches and instant cereals at supermarkets, pharmacies and drugstores. If you want organic food, look for the word "*Bio*".

- Pacifiers are very common and babies tend to drink from bottles for an extended period.

- Drugstores offer a range of baby products and have store club cards offering special deals.

Strollers

As you would in any city, keep an eye on your stroller and attached bags. Some stroller models are too wide to fit through the doors of the older trams and some building elevators, so check dimensions carefully before you buy. Carriers and baby slings also offer a good option for easy and quick travel around the city.

Activities for Children

Vienna is filled with fun places for children and families to explore. Start at Wienxtra-Kinderinfo in the *Museums Quartier*. You can sign up online for a free membership card and check out their calendar of events and activities.

Wienxtra – Kinderinfo
7, Museumplatz 1
8, Friedrich-Schmidt-Plz. 5
www.kinderinfowien.at

The **Vienna Tourism Board** offers up-to-date information on activities for kids: www.wien.info/en/vienna-for/families

Mamilade
Family and children's activities all around Austria, in German but easy to navigate. www.mamilade.at

Zoom Children's Museum (*Kindermuseum*)
More of a playroom than a museum in the traditional sense, with special exhibits by local and international artists, and interactive exhibits. Reservations are usually needed.
7, Museumplatz 1 (*Museums Quartier*)
www.kindermuseum.at

Dschungel Theater and Café
Next door to Zoom is a Children's Theater and baby and child friendly cafe.
7, Museumsplatz 1
www.dschungelwien.at

Aquarium (*Haus des Meeres*)
Located inside a WWII concrete air defense tower, with thousands of fish, animals and a tropical rainforest.
6, Esterhazypark
www.haus-des-meeres.at

Board Game Center (*Spielebox*)
Like a library for board games, with over 6,000 games in stock that can be played in the center for free or taken home for nominal fees.
8, Albertgasse 37
www.spielebox.at

Central Library (*Bucherei*)
The Vienna public library system runs an extensive children's program. A library card is free for children and branches are located throughout the city. Books and other

media are available in English and many other languages.
7, Urban-Loritz-Platz 2a
www.buechereien.wien.at

Cobenzl Petting Zoo and Playground
Working farm within the city limits and nearby forest
playground. Fantastic views of Vienna. Open year round.
19, Am Cobenzl 96a
www.landgutcobenzl.at

Digger Park
Kids can operate construction equipment.
11, Alberner Hafenzufahrtsstrasse 21
www.baggerpark.at

Indoor Playgrounds

When cold or rainy weather hits, many kids and parents
flock to large play complexes and neighborhood playrooms.
Most serve snacks and coffee, host birthday parties and
offer a good place to meet other parents. New locations
open all the time, so ask other parents or check with the
Vienna Babies Club and online: www.kinderinfowien.at

Imperial Vienna for Kids

Palace tours can be difficult for children; consider checking
out the special kid's tours, museums and activities. The
Kindermusuem at Schönbrunn does not require advance
reservations and allows kids to dress up in period costume.
The labyrinth and playground on the grounds are also fun.
The website www.kaiserkinder.at lists special children's
tours, including flashlight tours of the Imperial Apartments at

the Hofburg and a dress-up tour highlighting the beauty routine of Empress Elizabeth.

At the Marionette Theater at Schloss Schönbrunn, puppets perform full-length musicals. Shows last two - three hours and adults often attend, so children should be old enough to sit quietly for long periods. For schedule and information: www.marionettentheater.at

Museums

Many museums are free for children up to 18, but can be difficult for smaller children. The Natural History Museum, House of Music, and Technical Museum are great for the whole family and recommended for smaller children. The Wien Museum's free indoor playground is also popular in winter.

Prater

If you approach the Prater from the Praterstern U-Bahn station, you'll come to an amusement park with a tiny train, roller coasters, merry-go-rounds, pony rides, slides, bumper cars and of course the famous Ferris Wheel, the *Wiener Reisenrad.* Behind the amusement park, the "Green Prater" is a park that stretches on for several kilometers with wonderful playgrounds. A long recreation path stretches the entire length and is perfect for easy biking, in-line skating, jogging or just a stroll. You can find a trampoline and bouncy-house center, skateboarding area, swimming pool complex, duck ponds and wooded paths, two golf courses, two horse racing tracks, stables, a bowling alley, baseball fields, a field hockey center, and sandpits for volleyball.

Swimming

See the **Sports and Recreation** chapter for information on swimming pools.

Zoo

Schönbrunner Zoo (*Tiergarten*) is Europe's oldest and best zoo. An annual pass here is a good investment. In addition to visiting the animals, children enjoy the petting zoo and the playground. For information, see: **www.zoovienna.at**

Kids' Activities by Season

January - March
- Ice-skating at city hall (*Rathaus*)
- Carnival Parties (*Fasching*)
- Indoor Playgrounds

April - June
- Explore the Prater; rides open May 1 and a Children's Festival (*Kinderfest*) takes place in May
- Donauinsel Music Festival (late June)

July - August
- Beaches on the Old Danube (*Alte Donau*)
- Danube Island water playground (*Donauinsel Wasser Spielplatz*)
- Outdoor swimming pools such as *Stadionbad*

September - October

- Harvest Festival (*Erntedankfest*) at Heldenplatz
- Pumpkin Festivals (*Kurbisfest*)

November - December

- St Martin's Day, November 11
- St. Nicholas Day, December 6; St Nicholas brings oranges, treats and nuts to good children
- Christmas Markets offer treats, carnival rides and craft workshops for kids

Eating Out with Kids

Although few restaurants cater to children, children are welcome in almost all restaurants. Highchairs are often available on request however diaper changing facilities are harder to find. Some restaurants have playgrounds or children's corners. Special children's menus are rare, but Viennese food is very child-friendly and the all-day menus at cafes offer good options. Websites like Yelp and TripAdvisor can help identify whether a restaurant is child-friendly.

For recommendations near popular attractions, see: www.wien.info/en/vienna-for/families/child-friendly-restaurants

Children Glossary

acknowledgement of paternity	die Anerkennung der Vaterschaft
au pair **employment authorization**	die Zulassungsbestätigung für Au-pairs
Austrian labour authorities	das Arbeitsmarktservice, AMS
baby and children's clothing	die Kinderbekleidung
baby wipes	die Feuchttücher
bassinet	der Stubenwagen
bathtub	die Badewanne
birth certificate	die Geburtsurkunde
birth certificate of parents	die Geburtsurkunde der Eltern
breast pads	die Stilleinlagen
breastfeeding	das Stillen
changing table	der Wickeltisch
childcare benefit for stay-at-home moms	das Kinderbetreuungsgeld
contract of employment for an au-pair	der Au-Pair-Vertrag
cradle	die Wiege
crib, cot	das Gitterbett
diapers	die Windeln
employed woman	die Angestellte
family assistance	die Familienbeihilfe
fitted sheet	das Spannleintuch

high chair	der Hochstuhl, der Kindersitz
immunization	die Impfung
maternity clothes	die Umstandsmode
maternity leave benefit	das Wochengeld
monthly monetary benefit per child	die Familienbeihilfe
Mother-Child Passport	der Mutter-Kind Pass
pacifier	der Schnuller
parent-run private nurseries	die Kindergruppen
parents information center	die Elternberatungsstelle
personal appearance of father	die Anwesenheit des Vaters
playpen	die Gehschule
proof of parents nationality	der Staatsbürgerschaftsnachweis der Eltern
rubber crib mat	die Gummiunterlage
safety seat	der Autokindersitz
shopping bag	die Tragtasche
sling carrier	das Tragetuch
stay-at-home mothers	die Tagesmütter
stroller, pram	der Kinderwagen
supplementary private insurance	die Zusatzversicherung
toy stores	die Spielwarengeschäfte
travel bed	das Reisebett

Education

Photo Credit: Lenka Peugniez

9. EDUCATION

Good to know . . .

Consider Austrian schools. Immersion in a new language and culture can be the experience of a lifetime for your children. However, the education system may be different from yours, and your kids will need at least basic German.

Look into the international schools. English is the language of instruction, and students come from all over the world. For a list of English-speaking schools, see the US Embassy website: www.austria.usembassy.gov

There are many post-secondary education opportunities in Vienna for you and your older children, including the University of Vienna, accredited international colleges and universities, world-famous music schools and other schools offering classes of all kinds.

General information and resources are available at the Vienna Youth Information Center website: www.jugendinfowien.at

Preschool and Kindergarten

In Austria, children from ages 1 to 3 go to nursery school *(Krippe)*, from age 3 to 5, kindergarten *(Kindergarten)*; and from age 5 to 6, preschool *(Vorschule)*. For more information, see the ***Children*** chapter.

The following schools accept students at the beginning of the school year in mid-August. Places may be available at other times, so contact the schools to find out.

American International School (AIS)
Pre-kindergarten class (16 students) for 4-year-olds and two kindergarten classes (20 students each) for 5-year-olds. www.ais.at

Children's House
Located near the Vienna International Center, offers places for ages 1 to 6. www.montessori-vienna.at

Danube International School (DIS)
Maximum class size of 24 children, beginning at three years. www.danubeschool.com

International Christian School Vienna (ICSV)
Follows United States curriculum. www.icsv.at

Internationaler Kindergarten Arche Noah
Flexible hours adapted to parents' needs.
www.kindergartenarchenoah.at

International Montessori Pre-School
Offers half- and full-day programs for ages 3 to 6 and toddlers. www.montessori-preschool-vienna.com

Kids United International Kindergarten
Offers places for ages 1 to 6. www.kidsunited.at

Kindercompany
23 locations, bilingual groups. www.kindercompany.at

Privatkindergarten Alt Wien
At several locations, bilingual groups taught by native German and English speakers. www.alt-wien.at

Schmetterling Montessori Kindergarten
Two locations, offers bilingual groups. www.schmetterling.at

Spatzennest
Mixed-nationality early education from birth to age 6.
www.privat-kindergarten.com

United Children International Kindergarten
Native English-speaking teachers. www.unitedchildren.at

Vienna English Preschool (VEP)
Walking distance from the Vienna International Centre, a British school with a toddler group for ages 1-1/2 to 3 and a mixed group for ages 3 to 6.
www.viennaenglishpreschool.com

Vienna International School (VIS)
Four classes of 25 students each, for ages 3 to 5.
www.vis.ac.at

Primary and Secondary Schools

Austrian Schools

In Austria, all children must attend school for nine years, beginning at age six. Several different educational programs are available in the secondary schools, including specialized study in sciences, business and forestry. Ask for details from the schools.The goal of all secondary school education is the diploma (*Matura*), roughly equivalent to the US high school diploma.

If you consider enrolling your child in an Austrian school, keep in mind that the system is different from American and international schools. If your child cannot speak, read and write German, this may preclude some opportunities. Also, you and your child will need enough German to communicate with teachers and school administrators.

School Grade Comparison

Austria	US
die Volksschule	1st - 4th grade
die Hauptschule	5th - 8th grade (general studies)
die höhere Schule	9th - 12th or 13th grade (general, academic and vocational studies)

For more information about public and private Austrian and international schools in Vienna, see:
www.wien.gv.at/english/education/sulsystem.htm
or contact the city's Board of Education (*Stadtschulrat für Wien*): www.stadtschulrat.at

Bilingual Schools

Bilingual schooling (*bilinguale Schule* or *zweisprachige Schule*) is available at many schools in Vienna. The city's Board of Education has programs to prepare students for a globalized economy, with language learning from first grade and bilingual instruction through secondary school. Vienna Bilingual Schooling (VBS) is based on the Austrian curriculum (*Lehrplan*) and designed for German- and English-speaking students. Native speakers teach the classes.

Currently there are ten VBS primary schools and ten VBS secondary schools. As demand for bilingual and international programs grows, the city is increasing the number of VBS schools. For more information, contact the City School Inspector's office for bilingual education.

English-Instruction Schools

AMADEUS – International School Vienna
AMADEUS International School Vienna (K-12), founded in 2012, offers academic education and training in classical music. The program is based on the International Baccalaureate (IB) curriculum. Participation in the music program is mandatory, but primary students can enter without prior music education. Secondary students should have studied an instrument for at least two years. Offers on-campus boarding. www.amadeus-vienna.com

American International School (AIS)
AIS is an independent, co-educational day school, with an elementary school (pre-K - grade 5), middle school (grade 6 - 8), and high school (grade 9 - 12). Curriculum and teaching methods follow the American system. Instruction is in English, with a comprehensive German curriculum in all grades; French and Spanish are introduced in middle school. Offers US high school diploma, International Baccalaureate (IB) and the Austrian Matura. www.ais.at

Danube International School (DIS)
DIS has a sports hall, theater, science laboratories, computer center, library and an arts center. Students may enroll at age five and continue through the IB. DIS may recommend additional instruction in English prior to

admission, but your child does not need a high level of English to apply. www.danubeschool.com

International Christian School Vienna (ICSV)
ICSV was founded to educate children of missionaries in Vienna and the surrounding area. Since 1994, enrollment is open to the international community for kindergarten through grade 12. ICSV is accredited with the Association of Christian Schools International. www.icsv.at

Vienna Elementary School (VES)
VES offers a comprehensive elementary school program in English from kindergarten - grade 4. English is the language of instruction; the curriculum combines Austrian and American systems. In 2012, the Vienna European School opened for students from ages 10 – 18 with an Austrian Matura program. www.vienna-elementary-school.at

Vienna International School (VIS)
VIS is an accredited international school with grades 1-12. Instruction is in English, with a comprehensive German program. Children can also study French, Spanish and English as a Second Language, as well as prepare for the IB and the Austrian Matura. www.vis.ac.at

University Studies

In Austrian universities, students declare a major at the beginning of their studies. For more information on public and private universities in Vienna, see: www.wien.gv.at/english/education/tertiary-education

Business and Technical School
Fachhochschule für Wirtschaft und Technik
The Business and Technical School in Wiener Neustadt, south of Vienna, offers a Business Consultancy degree program in English. Students must complete an internship in an English-speaking country or an international company where English is the working language. www.fhwn.ac.at

Institute of European Studies (IES)
IES is a consortium of 135 US colleges and universities that offers a semester or academic year abroad for sophomores, juniors, and seniors. IES offers music, art, literature, psychology, history, political science, economics and business courses in English and German. www.iesabroad.org/study-abroad/vienna

Open University Business School
The Open University Business School is Europe's largest business school with more than 30,000 students, accredited by the European Foundation for Management Development. www.openuniversity.edu

Sigmund Freud University
Sigmund Freud University offers psychotherapy training including psychoanalysis, Gestalt therapy and systemic family therapy. They have an in-house outpatient clinic, providing psychotherapy services in German and English. www.sfu.ac.at

Tourism College MODUL (MU)
MU offers an English-language diploma course to secondary school graduates (*Matura*) or equivalent. There

are twenty-five students per class and a network of graduates from over 50 countries. The program offers hotel management, cooking, service and front office management. www.modul.at

Webster University
Webster University, based in St. Louis, Missouri, is an accredited American university offering day and evening B.A., B.S., M.A. and M.B.A. programs in English, in international relations, management, computer science, psychology and other areas in small-classroom settings. www.webster.ac.at

To find more information on post-secondary education in Austria:
- www.studieren.at
- www.wien.gv.at/english/education
- www.oeh.ac.at

English Teaching

Accredited language schools in Vienna expect English teachers to have TOEFL, CELTA or a similar teaching certificate if they do not have a university degree in language education. Current European Union labor law makes it difficult for teachers who are not EU citizens to get working visas in Austria. A few organizations offer online and on-site programs that qualify you for a position as an English native speaker teacher.

Language Teaching to Adults (CELTA)
www.cambridgeenglish.org/exams-and-qualifications/

Teachers of English as a Foreign Language (TOEFL)
www.ets.org/portal/toefl

TEFL Corporation
www.teflcorp.com

Adult and Continuing Education

Vienna's Adult Education Centers (*Volkshochschulen*) offer a variety of courses, most taught in German. Call or e-mail to request a catalog. The website provides a listing of all courses offered in VHS schools in each district of Vienna. See: www.vhs.at

Music Education

University for Music and Performing Arts of Vienna
Formerly known as the Vienna Academy of Music, this is one of the world's most renowned music schools. They offer two degree programs: the Austrian Masters of Arts and Doctorate program, and post-graduate studies. They also offer a youth program (*Vorbereitungskurs für Kinder/ Jugendliche*) for children age 6 to 17. www.mdw.ac.at

Conservatory Vienna
This is a private university offering B.A. and M.A. degrees. There are 12 departments, including music pedagogy, jazz, acting and ballet. www.konservatorium-wien.ac.at

Other private conservatories include:

Prayner Conservatory for Music and Dramatic Arts
Offers Bachelor and Master of Arts degrees.
www.konservatorium-prayner.at

Franz Schubert Conservatory
Offers courses for amateur musicians *(Hobbymusiker)*.
www.fsk.at

Gustav Mahler Conservatorium for Music and Dramatic Arts www.mahler-konservatorium.at

Education Glossary

Bachelor of Arts	der Bachelor of Arts (B.A.)
Bachelor of Science	der Bachelor of Science (B.Sc.)
bilingual	bilingual, zweisprachig
class	die Klasse
course	der Kurs
curriculum	der Lehrplan
Doctorate, Ph.D.	der Doktor
education	die Ausbildung
foreign language	die Fremdsprache
high school	die höhere Schule, das Gymnasium
high school diploma	die Matura
kindergarten	die Vorschule
language course	der Deutschkurs
language school	die Sprachschule
Master of Arts	der Magister (Mag.)
Master of Science	der Diplom-Ingenieur (Dipl. Ing.)
middle/high school	das Gymnasium
nursery school	die Krippe
preschool	der Kindergarten
primary school	die Volksschule
teacher	der Lehrer, die Lehrerin
university	die Universität
Vienna School Board	der Stadtschulrat Wien

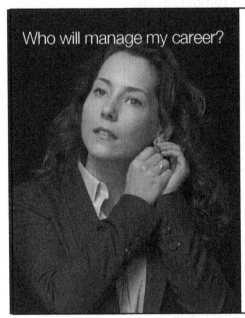

Health Care

Photo Credit: Jerry Barton

10. HEALTH CARE

Good to know . . .

Call 144 for an ambulance if you have a medical emergency. See *In Case of Emergency* at the back of this book for a complete list of emergency phone numbers.

Ambulance in German is *"Rettung"* not *"Ambulanz"*, which means an outpatient clinic.

Locate the hospital and pharmacy nearest your home. Learn the fastest route to get there in an emergency.

Get a pharmacy after-hours calendar (*Nachtdienstkalender*) from your local pharmacist so you know which pharmacies are open after-hours and on weekends.

Alternative medicine is available in Austria, sometimes integrated with conventional medicine, and practiced by licensed medical professionals.

Medical reports are your responsibility so keep test results, lab and doctors' reports and x-rays. Take them with you when you go for follow-up medical visits and annual physical exams.

Carry your e-card and any other insurance cards with you at all times. If you're pregnant, carry your Mother-Child Passport (*Mutter-Kind Pass*).

Emergency Resources

For a handy reference of emergency telephone numbers, see *In Case of Emergency*. For a list of medical terms, see the Health Care Glossary.

Ambulances

When you call 144 for an ambulance, the driver may not take you to the nearest hospital. Unless your doctor has been notified and has specified a hospital, the ambulance driver will be told by a central dispatcher where the patient should be admitted. There is a charge for emergency and urgent transportation services.

If you suspect that someone is having a heart attack *(Herzanfall)*, tell the dispatcher when you call. A physician and staff trained in cardiac emergency care will arrive in the ambulance. Here are a few sentences to remember when you call for an ambulance:

I need an ambulance.	*Ich brauche einen Krankenwagen.*
My address is...	*Meine Adresse ist...*
My name is...	*Mein Name ist...*
My telephone number is...	*Meine Telefonnummer ist...*

Accidental Poisoning

In case of suspected poisoning, call the poison center and state clearly what was ingested, if you know, and how much. Save the container of suspected poison to show the doctor.

Poison Center *(Die Vergiftungsinformationszentrale VIZ)*
+43 1 406 4343
This is a 24-hour service, available seven days a week. English-speaking physicians are available.

Accidents

If you are injured and your doctor is not available, go directly to an emergency room or trauma center *(Unfallspital)*. If your injury isn't serious enough to require an ambulance, take a taxi. Taxi drivers know the fastest routes and the appropriate hospital entrance, and you won't have to deal with traffic and parking. To find the emergency room or trauma center nearest you, look under *Krankenhäuser* or *Unfallspitäler*.

Children's Emergencies

If your child is ill or injured and your doctor is unavailable, take your child to an emergency room or trauma center. If you prefer, you can take your child to the emergency room of a pediatric hospital *(Kinderklinik)*.

After-Hours Medical Care

When your doctor is unavailable, there are several services you can contact.

Doctors-on-Call *(Ärztefunkdienst)*
A doctor comes to your home, examines the patient and prescribes medication, if necessary. You can request an English-speaking doctor.
Dial 141

On-Duty Dentists *(Zahnarztbereitschaft)*
A recording in German gives the names and telephone numbers of dentists on emergency call in each district.
+43 1 512 2078

Crises
Crisis counseling is available from:

Social Hotline Vienna (*Sozialruf Wien*)
This hotline offers information and counseling services on home nursing, family matters and disabilities. The website provides resource addresses.
+43 1 533 7777
www.sozialruf.wien.gv.at

Social Psychiatric Emergency Service
(*Sozialpsychiatrische Notdienst*)
A 24-hour service for mental health emergencies and crisis situations. Phone, outpatient and mobile services are available.
+43 1 310 8779
www.psd-wien.at

Women's Emergency Hotline (*Frauennotruf*)
24-hour counseling and crisis intervention for women and girls threatened or affected by sexual, physical or psychological harm. Providing medical, psychological, social and legal help.
+43 1 717 19
www.wien.gv.at/menschen/frauen/servicestellen/
frauennotruf.html

Pharmacies

A pharmacy (*Apotheke*) can be found in every neighborhood in Vienna. You can buy prescription and most non-prescription drugs there, including aspirin and cough syrup.

Look for the red "A" or green cross symbols.

Contrary to its name, a drugstore (*Drogerie*) does not sell drugs; it sells personal care and household goods.

After-hours Pharmacy

In each district, pharmacies rotate the overnight and weekend shift. You can find a list of the nearest open pharmacies posted outside every closed pharmacy, at the local police station and in the weekend newspapers. Ask your pharmacist for a *Nachtdienstkalender* for a full list of all-night pharmacies.

During non-standard opening times, you have to ring or knock on the door for a pharmacist to serve you through a small window in the door. You pay an extra charge for pharmacy purchases after hours.

After-hours Pharmacy Service
Apotheken-Bereitschaftsdienst
A recording in German of the pharmacies on duty.
+43 1 155 0

Prescription Delivery Service

If you are unable to go to a pharmacy and need to have a prescription filled, you can call the Workers' Samaritan Union's prescription delivery service (*Medikamentenzustelldienst*). For €22 a representative picks up the prescription and money from your home, goes to the nearest open pharmacy, and brings you your medicine.

Medical Insurance

The Austrian national health insurance system (*Krankenkasse - KK*) insures every Austrian citizen. About 15% of people residing in Austria have private medical insurance (*Nebenversicherung* or *Zusatzversicherung*) in addition to national health insurance, or as their only form of insurance.

Austrian National Health Insurance

Austrian health insurance is part of a comprehensive social security system (*Sozialversicherung*) that includes accident insurance, workmen's compensation and pensions. The health insurance system is a national umbrella organization, with several smaller groups (*Kassen*) based on geography or occupation. Most people who have Austrian national health insurance in Vienna are insured by the Vienna Health Insurance Agency (*Wiener Gebietskrankenkasse - WGKK*). Participation in Austrian national health insurance is mandatory for everyone working in Austria with a standard employment contract and for those who have a commercial license (*Gewerbeschein*). The premium for coverage is a fixed percentage of a person's salary, half paid by the employee and half by the employer.

Every permanent resident of Austria can be insured under the Austrian national health insurance. You can apply at the Health Insurance Agency (*Gebietskrankenkasse*). If you are self-employed, unemployed or in school, this is called self-insurance (*Selbstversicherung*). For more information, contact your employer or the WGKK.

Wiener Gebietskrankenkasse

Foreign residents working for international organizations may have automatic coverage for themselves and for their family from their organization's own private medical insurance plan. United Nations and other international organization employees can choose between Austrian national health insurance and private health insurance. www.wgkk.at

The e-card System

The European Health Insurance Card (EHIC) called the e-card is the standard health insurance card in Austria. The e-card is a smart card with an embedded computer chip that replaces paper medical referrals. It supports administrative processes between health-insured individuals, medical providers, employers and social security agencies. You receive the e-card at no cost from your health insurance provider.

The front of the e-card displays administrative information, including your name, health insurance number, gender and user group identification.

The back of the e-card replaces the European Union's health insurance voucher previously used for claiming medical expenses in EEA countries and Switzerland.

For further information, go to www.chipkarte.at and click *English information*.

Medical Vouchers

If you do not have an e-card, when you visit your doctor, you use a voucher (*Krankenschein*), which you get from your employer or from your national health insurance office if you are self-insured. There are three types of vouchers, each issued quarterly, for:

- general practitioners
- specialists
- dentists

You present your voucher at your initial visit to the doctor. It entitles you to three months of unlimited visits to the doctor. You cannot change doctors during the three months. However, you can see a new doctor at the beginning of the new quarter, when you can get a new voucher.

If your doctor goes on vacation during the quarter, he/she will arrange for a colleague (usually one with an office nearby) to see his/her patients during that time. You do not need an additional voucher to see this doctor. If you go on vacation in Austria during the three-month period, you can request a vacation voucher (*Urlaubsüberweisung*) so that you can see another physician during your trip.

Specialist Referrals

If your doctor refers you to a specialist or for a medical test, you will be given a medical referral voucher (*Überweisungsschein*). Present this voucher for treatment within two weeks of the date of issue.

If you do not bring a voucher with you, your doctor will either ask you to pay a deposit (*Einlage*) of €40, or ask you to sign a form promising to submit a voucher within a set number of days. You do not need a voucher for emergency treatment, for an ambulance, or for the Doctors-on-Call service.

Krankenkasse Benefits

In addition to doctor's visits, you have other benefits under the national health insurance system, including:

- annual physical examination
- hospital treatment
- parental leave
- medical and therapeutic devices
- medication
- compensation during sick leave
- treatment in other countries

Private Medical Insurance

Some Austrians have private insurance in addition to national health insurance to cover additional benefits or costs such as special care (*Sonderklasse*) in a hospital, or a consultation by a private doctor who doesn't accept national health insurance. There are many Austrian insurance firms that provide such coverage, either as part of a group insurance plan organized by an employer, or as an individual plan. For information on private insurance, talk to your employer or search *Krankenversicherung*.

Medical Coverage Abroad

Take your e-card with you when you travel in Europe. EEA countries and Switzerland have reciprocal healthcare agreements with Austria. If you have Austrian national health insurance and become ill or have an accident while traveling, present your e-card to receive care under the local country's healthcare system. If you do not have an e-card, you need a certificate for foreign care (*Auslandsbetreuungsschein*), which you get from your employer or from the national health insurance office before you leave Austria.

If you have private health insurance, check your policy for coverage restrictions when leaving the country.

Insurance at Home

If your employer sends you to Austria as an expatriate, ask about the impact on your coverage under the corporate insurance plan in your home country. Questions to ask include:

- Can you continue your insurance as an individual?
- If you stay abroad longer than originally intended, can you continue your insurance?
- What if you leave your job?
- Can your family members be insured on your policy if they do not accompany you abroad?

Health Insurance is not Universal

Doctors, clinics and other health-service have different policies concerning which health insurance plans are accepted. *"Alle Kassen"* means the doctor accepts all Austrian health insurance. *"Keine Kassen"* means he/she consults patients only on a private-payment basis. If you go to a doctor who does not accept your insurance, you must pay for the consultation yourself, usually in cash before you leave the office, or have a private health plan pay for it.

Expatriate Insurance

Depending on your specific circumstances and insurance coverage, expatriate medical insurance may be a good choice. Expatriate medical insurance policies usually offer home country treatment and, in case of a critical medical condition, arrangements for medically necessary evacuation or repatriation. This type of insurance reimburses travel and accommodation expenses that arise due to an emergency in your home country such as critical illness or death of a family member. Travel insurance policies sometimes include this service.

General exclusions may exist for fertility treatment, elective cosmetic surgery and pre-existing conditions. Most insurers consider pregnancy a pre-existing condition. Insurers vary on their coverage of chronic conditions.

If you are transferred to Vienna with a job, employers often can provide advice. If you come to Austria on your own, expatriate health insurance may meet the Austrian authorities' requirement that you have health insurance to reside legally in the country. There are insurance companies in Vienna that specialize in expat health insurance for groups such as UN employees.

For more information, see:

- americansabroad.org
- www.aaro.org
- www.clements.com
- www.goodhealthworldwide.com

US Medicare

The Medicare system covers US citizens only when they travel to Canada or Mexico. Check your Medicare supplement to find details on your overseas coverage. In addition, advise family members who rely on Medicare benefits to consider travel health insurance before they visit.

Doctors

You can choose your general practitioner (*Allgemeinmediziner, Praktische Arzt*). Your general practitioner often chooses your specialists.

If you consult a doctor who does not accept your Austrian national health insurance, and he orders lab tests and X-rays, ask your general practitioner to rewrite the prescriptions. Your insurance will then cover the costs. Also, you can submit your receipts for the doctor's fees to the national health insurance for possible partial reimbursement.

A personal recommendation from a trusted source is a good way to find a doctor. Here are official sources that can help you locate a doctor who will best match your needs and expectations.

Vienna Chamber of Doctors (*Ärztekammer für Wien*)
The Vienna Chamber of Doctors, also known as the Vienna Medical Association, has an online database of all doctors registered in Vienna. To search for a doctor, click "*Praxisplan*". Then you can search by several different criteria, including specialty (*Fachgebiet*), postal code (*Postleitzahl*), and languages spoken (*Sprachen*). If you want a private doctor, select "*keine*", for insurance accepted (*Krankenkassen*). To start your search, click "*Suchen*". This is a very quick way of finding, for example, all English-speaking obstetricians in the district where you live. www.aekwien.at

Department for Foreign Patients
(*Servicestelle für ausländische Patienten*)
This service of the Vienna Chamber of Doctors, specifically for foreign patients, provides free information about types and length of treatment and prospective costs. It can also help you find a doctor or specialist who speaks English. Emails are answered within 48 hours. For a downloadable brochure, see: www.aekwien.at/media/foreignpatient.pdf or www.aekwien.at/index.php/hotlines-a-patienteninfo/ auslaend-patienten

Doctor Listings

Your country's consulate or embassy may have a list of doctors who speak English. You can find the US Embassy's list of doctors at www.austria.usembassy.gov/doctors.html If you are a UN employee or spouse of an employee, check with the United Nations Medical Service for more information and referrals. If you have children who attend private school in Vienna, their school may have a list of recommended doctors.

To find a dentist (*Zahnarzt*), contact:

* **Austrian Dentists Association**
  Österreichische Zahnärztekammer
  www.zahnaerztekammer.at

Medical Appointments

You can either make an appointment with your doctor or walk in during regular consultation hours *(Ordination)*. If you do not have an appointment, your doctor will see you on a first-come-first-served basis, so be prepared to wait.

In Austria, doctors do not offer examination gowns to their patients, nor are nurses usually present during an exam. If you are uncomfortable without a gown, bring your own or wear a long slip. When your doctor says "*Bitte, machen Sie sich frei*", it is a request to disrobe.

House Calls

Many Austrian doctors still make house calls outside normal office hours. Even if the examination at home is covered by your insurance, the doctor can charge a fee for a house call.

Annual Medical Check-up

If you have Austrian national health insurance and are age 19 or older, you can have a free annual preventive medical check-up (*Vorsorgeuntersuchung*). The check-up is by appointment with contracted doctors or at any one of five check-up centers in Vienna.

These are the tests performed during the check-up:
- blood test
- urine analysis
- scatoscopy (testing for occult blood)
- body fat analysis
- pulmonary function test
- electrocardiogram
- internal diagnosis
- blood pressure
- ear, nose and throat examination
- hearing test
- gynecological examination and Pap test for women
- strength test

For a list of check-up centers, see: www.wien.gv.at/english/health-socialservices/preventive.html

Alternative Treatments

Alternative and complementary therapies are widely available in Austria and are often incorporated in standard medical practices. In Austria, only medical doctors are permitted to diagnose and prescribe treatment or conduct an invasive procedure.

Massage Therapy

Many different types of massage therapy are available in Vienna, including therapeutic, Swedish, Shiatsu, acupressure, polarity and reflexology. Massage therapists are often skilled in a variety of techniques to meet the varying needs of their clients. Traditional Chinese Medicine and many homeopathic practices incorporate some form of massage therapy.

Homeopathy

There is an element of homeopathy in many modern Austrian medical practices. To find a homeopathic specialist, search for *Homöopathie.*

See also: Austrian Society of Homeopathic Medicine www.homoeopathie.at

Acupuncture

Only medical doctors are allowed to practice acupuncture (*Akupunktur*) in Austria. Recommendations for English-speaking practitioners can be found at: Traditional Chinese Medicine Academy www.tcm-academy.org

Immunization and Vaccinations

Most vaccinations (*Impfungen*) recommended by the Austrian National Health Board are free for children up to age 15. If you have questions about required vaccinations for your child, ask your general practitioner, pediatrician or school nurse. Your local Parents Information Center (*Elternberatungsstelle*) can also provide information. To find the center in your district see: www.wien.gv.at/menschen/magelf/service/elternberatungen.html

Tick-Borne Encephalitis

In parts of Austria, including Vienna and the Vienna Woods, there is a risk of contracting tick-borne encephalitis (TBE). Austria has developed a highly effective vaccine against TBE. If you live in Vienna and surrounding areas and participate in outdoor activities in areas known to have tick populations, you should be vaccinated. TBE immunizations (*Zeckenschutzimpfungen*) are a series of three injections, usually given in the late winter or early spring. See your general practitioner for more information.

Some international school nurses administer the TBE vaccine to students for a fee. Some employers arrange for a nurse to come and administer the vaccine to interested employees.

If you get bitten . . .
If a tick bites you, and you have not been immunized, contact a doctor immediately. If left untreated, you risk contracting encephalitis.

Travel Abroad

A medical office provides information on recommended immunizations for various travel destinations. Most vaccinations are held in stock. Make sure to take details of any previous vaccinations you have had.

Vaccination Service and Foreign Travel Advice
(*Impfservice und reisemedizinsche Beratung*)
www.wien.gv.at/gesundheit/beratung-vorsorge/impfen/
beratung/

Tropical Disease Center (*Tropenzentrum*)
For vaccines and treatment of tropical illnesses. Private
patients only. www.tropencentersued.at

Hospitals

Vienna has many hospitals, both public and private.
Austrian authorities classify a hospital (*Krankenhaus*) by its
care, either general (*Allgemeine Klasse*) or special
(*Sonderklasse*). Your doctor determines your hospital if you
have a non-emergency admission; this may be important for
expectant mothers. The quality of medical care is the same
for both, but you may consider a stay at a special hospital
more comfortable.

A general hospital admits patients who have Austrian
national health insurance or who are from a country with a
treaty with Austria, including EU countries. Wards vary in
size, visiting hours are restricted, and your doctor is the
doctor on duty.

A special hospital has private visiting hours, personal care
and a choice of doctors. Typically, there are two patients per
room, each with a television set with headphones, shared
bathroom facilities and selection of meals. Most private
insurance plans cover the cost for a stay in a special
hospital. However, unless you also have Austrian national

health insurance, at admission you may be required to make a substantial deposit toward the cost of your stay.

Take all health insurance cards with you to the hospital, including your e-card. You may want to bring a German-English dictionary too.

For hospitals in Vienna, see the listing in the back of this chapter or see:
www.wien.gv.at/english/health-socialservices/hospitals/

Trauma Centers
Each of the following public hospitals has a trauma center *(Unfallspital)*.

Allgemeines Krankenhaus (AKH)
9, Währinger Gürtel 18-20
+43 1 404 0019 64

University of Vienna
Unfallkrankenhaus Meidling
12, Kundratstr. 37
+43 1 601 50

Lorenz Böhler Unfallkrankenhaus
20, Donaueschingenstr. 13
+43 1 331 10

Sozialmedizinisches Zentrum Ost
22, Langobardenstr. 122
+43 1 288 020

Krankenanstalt Rudolfstiftung
3, Juchg. 25
+43 1 711 650

Wilhelminenspital
16, Montleartstr. 37
+43 1 491 500

Hanusch-Krankenhaus
14, Heinrich-Collin-Str. 30
+43 1 910 21

Pediatric Facilities:

Krankenanstalt Rudolfstiftung
3, Juchg. 25
+43 1 716 5261 1

St.-Anna-Kinderspital
9, Kinderspitalg. 6
+43 1 401 7022 4

Gottfried von Preyerisches Kinderspital
10, Schrankenbergg. 31
+43 1 601 13

Vienna General Hospital
(Universitätsklinik für Kinder- und Jugendheilkunde)
9, Währinger Gürtel 18-20
+43 1 404 0032 29

Wilhelminenspital
(Notfallambulanz der Internen Kinderabteilung)
17, Flötzersteig 4
+43 1 491 5029 11

Donauspital im SMZ Ost
(Kinderambulanz)
22, Langobardenstr. 122
+43 1 288 0243 50

Women's Health

The area of women's health alone could make up an entire book. Here we've provided some contacts and resources. To find a gynecologist (*Frauenarzt* or *Facharzt für Frauenheilkunde*) or an obstetrician (*Geburtshelfer* or *Facharzt für Geburtshilfe*), see "Doctors."

Women Advising Women
Frauen Beraten Frauen
Offers counseling, legal and health-related advice and psychotherapy: www.frauenberatenfrauen.at

Pregnancy Termination

Abortion is legal in Austria. Every woman is free to decide whether she wants to keep her baby until the third month of pregnancy. Specialized hospitals, some gynecologists' offices and certain public hospitals perform abortions. Austrian national health insurance does not cover this procedure.

Fertility Services

More than 20 specialized hospitals throughout Austria offer assisted reproduction. In certain cases, costs are partly covered by the Austrian IVF Fund (*IVF-Fonds*). Speak with your fertility specialist for more information. These hospitals offer fertility services:

Allgemeines Krankenhaus der Stadt Wien
www.akhwien.at

Goldenes Kreuz
www.kinderwunschzentrum.at

Kinderwunschzentrum Gynandron
www.sterilitaet.at

Krankenhaus Hietzing
www.lainz.at

Wunschbaby-Zentrum
www.wunschbaby.at

Pregnancy

If you are pregnant (*schwanger*) and plan to have a baby in Vienna, contact the Vienna Babies Club (see the chapters *Social Networks* and *Children*). This support group for new and expectant mothers holds regular informal meetings where pregnant women and mothers with babies can share experiences and information. Many members may have given birth recently, so their recommendations of doctors and hospitals, advice on pregnancy, delivery and breastfeeding are current. For more information: www.viennababiesclub.com.

The Mother-Child Passport

If you are pregnant, make your first appointment with your obstetrician, including a blood test, before your 16th week. Your doctor will give you a Mother-Child Passport (*Mutter-Kind Pass*) and record all examinations, including details of the birth, and immunizations until age 5. Carry this document with you at all times; it can save lives in an emergency. Austrian national health insurance covers the cost of these examinations.

You may want to familiarize yourself with the childhood immunization schedule of your home country; it may differ from Austria. There may be immunizations that are not standard here, and are not included in your insurance coverage such as the vaccine against chicken pox.

Maternity Hospitals

Most hospitals welcome expectant parents, and will give you a tour of their maternity wards. Call ahead for visiting hours. Hospitals in Austria may not offer the same services or privacy you might desire. For example, there will usually not be curtains between beds in shared rooms. In addition, not all hospitals in Austria are air-conditioned, which may affect your choice if your due date is in the summer.

Hospital Registration

Most hospitals require you to register your intention to give birth there when you are 20 weeks pregnant. A few hospitals require you to register as early as 12 weeks in advance.

Public Hospitals for Births

If you have Austrian public health insurance, you can deliver at a public hospital at no charge. The doctor on duty delivers your baby and your room and bathroom are shared. If you have private health insurance, you can also receive care in a public hospital. As a private patient you can choose from the doctors at the hospital and will have a single room. Contact your private insurance provider to verify what it covers. Here are some public hospitals in Vienna with birthing facilities:

Ignaz Semmelweis Frauenklinik
Provides experienced midwives, with a doctor on duty in case of complications. Known for its natural approach to birthing.
18, Bastieng. 36
+43 1 01 476 1557 71

Universitäts-Frauenklinik
Part of Allgemeines Krankenhaus (AKH), the largest hospital in Vienna. Offers neo-natal emergency care, often making it the choice for women with high-risk pregnancies.
9, Währinger-Gürtel 18
+43 1 404 0028 22

St. Josef Wien-Hacking
Roman Catholic hospital run by nuns; most do not speak English, but the doctors do.
13, Auhofstr. 189
43 1 878 44

Private Hospitals for Births

You can choose to give birth in a private hospital based on your obstetrician's affiliations. You will have a private room with a bathroom. However, you may have to pay part of its cost.

Goldenes Kreuz

A popular private hospital with English-speaking staff. Neo-natal care is available at the nearby Allgemeines Krankenhaus (AKH) and University Children's Hospital.
9, Lazarettg. 16
43 1 401 1154 0

Privatklinik Döbling

9, Heiligenstädterstr. 57
+43 1 360 660

Rudolfinerhaus

Some English-speaking staff.
19, Billrothstr. 78
+43 1 360 36

Home Births

Home births are not as common in Austria as in other parts of the world, but they are possible. There are several independent midwives (*Hebamme* or *Geburtshelferin*) in the Vienna area, including a few who speak English. Your midwife helps you prepare for the birth during regular prenatal visits. She will be on call for your delivery and will deliver and register the baby. Your midwife will then check on you and the baby daily for seven to ten days after the birth.

If a hospital visit is necessary, midwives can accompany you only to the hospitals where they are able to practice. Some midwives accept Austrian national health insurance. Check with your doctor or at your local parent-child center for information on practicing midwives in your area. Or you can contact one of these organizations:

NANAYA

Provides counseling in pregnancy issues, including natural childbirth and life with children.
7, Zollerg. 37
+43 1 523 1711
www.nanaya.at

Hebammenzentrum

9, Lazarettg. 6/2/1
+43 1 408 8022
www.hebammenzentrum.at

Epidurals

If you want to have an epidural, discuss this in advance with your doctor or hospital. Practices vary; epidurals may not be available at all hospitals.

Maternity Hospital Stays

Hospital stays in Austria may be longer than in your home country. The standard is about five days; longer for a Caesarean. Remain in the hospital for the recommended period, particularly for your first child. There is no formal support structure for home visits or baby clinics in Austria.

An ambulatory delivery is possible. The hospital will discharge you and your baby six hours after delivery, provided that you have arranged for a midwife to visit you at home. Hospitals usually offer baby care courses during your stay, as well as support such as breastfeeding assistance.

Rooming-in

Rooming-in, or having your baby stay in your room, at all times, with nurses ready to assist, is typical in Austrian hospitals. Ask how many mothers and babies will be in a room with you as it can vary between hospitals. Check the hospital's visitation policy. Most have strict rules concerning who may visit, when and for how long. These rules apply to fathers and siblings.

Prenatal Classes

Most hospitals offer both prenatal-exercise and birth-preparation classes in German. The exercise classes usually cover breathing and relaxation techniques as well as birthing positions. Even if your German is limited, consider attending these classes.

Infant Care

A pediatrician is not normally present at the delivery, but will examine your baby shortly afterwards. He then performs a complete pediatric examination within a few days after birth. You may want to look for a pediatrician before your baby is born. Your hospital or obstetrician may be able to give you referrals.

Circumcision

Hospitals rarely perform circumcision (*Beschneidung*) in Austria. If you would like your baby boy to be circumcised, tell your doctor before the birth so that appropriate arrangements can be made.

Men's Health

Awareness and research in the area of men's health (*Männergesundheit*) in Austria are developing, so you can find many skilled professionals and reliable information on men's physical and psychological healthcare. To find a doctor specializing in andrology, dealing with male erectile dysfunction and hormonal disorders, search for a urologist (*Urologe*): www.aekwien.at/index.php/hotlines-a-patienteninfo/auslaend-patienten

Men's Center
An information and advisory center with an English-speaking staff: www.men-center.at

Elderly and Disabled Care Resources

As in many cities, it can be difficult to get around Vienna in a wheelchair (*Rollstuhl*). The Vienna public transit system is working toward becoming barrier free. For information on accessibility on bus lines and *U-Bahn* stations, see www.wl-barrierefrei.at. There are kneeling buses and kneeling trams, as well as many low-floor trams.

You can find information about accessibility, including disabled parking permits (*Behindertenausweis*) and parking places (*Behindertenparkplatz*) at: www.wien.gv.at/sozialinfo/content/en/10/DirectoryDetail.do?liid=7

In addition you can find details about travel on public transportation, accessibility at the airport and train stations, wheelchair rental, transportation services, tour guides, accessible public restrooms and accessible housing.

There are a number of public, public-assisted and private organizations providing counseling, advice and services for the elderly and disabled and their caregivers. Here are a few resources:

Federal Social Welfare Department *Bundesozialamt*
Provides information about care, subsidies, and other services for the elderly and disabled: www.basb.gv.at

Ministry of Social Affairs and Consumer Protection
Advises the elderly or disabled, their relatives and professional caregivers, including information on long-term care benefits: www.bmsk.gv.at

Senior Citizens Bureau of the City of Vienna
Seniorenbüro der Stadt Wien: www.senior-in-wien.at

BIZEPS *Behindertenberatungszentrum*
Provides information for people with special needs: www.bizeps.or.at

Here are two organizations offering support to the blind, visually impaired, deaf and hearing impaired:

Austrian Union for the Blind and Visually Impaired
Österreichischer Blinden- und Sehbehindertenverband: www.oebsv.at

Austrian Association for the Hearing Impaired
Österreichischer Gehörlosenbund: www.oeglb.at

Healthcare Disputes

The Vienna Healthcare and Patient Advocate (*Wiener Pflege-, Patientinnen- und Patientenanwaltschaft - WPPA*) is an independent group that deals with healthcare disputes, provides information about patient rights and home healthcare, and provides mediation. Services are at no cost.

Vienna Healthcare and Patient Advocate

(*Patientenanwaltschaft*)
www.wien.gv.at/gesundheit/einrichtungen/
patientenanwaltschaft

Austrian Red Cross Blood Donor Center

(*Blutspendezentrale des Österreichischen Roten Kreuzes*)
English is spoken.
4, Wiedner-Hauptstr. 30
+43 1 589 000

AIDS Help Vienna

AIDS Hilfe Wien
Provides advice, support and information on HIV and AIDS:
www.aids.at

Pollen Alert Service

(*Pollenwarndienst*)
Provides pollen forecasts, alerts and information on allergies: www.pollenwarndienst.at

Workers' Samaritan Union

Arbeiter Samariter Bund
+43 1 891 44

Public and Private Hospitals in Vienna by District

denotes private hospital

2nd District
Krankenhaus Barmherzige Brüder*
2, Grosse Mohreng. 9
+43 1 211 210
www.barmherzige-brueder.at/wien

3rd District
Krankenhaus Rudolfsstiftung
3, Juchg. 25
+43 1 711 650

9th District
Allgemeines Krankenhaus (AKH)
Vienna General Hospital
9, Währinger Gürtel 18-20
+43 1 404 000
www.akhwien.at

Goldenes Kreuz*
9, Lazarettg. 16
+43 1 401 110
www.goldenes-kreuz.at

St. Anna Kinderspital
pediatric hospital
9, Kinderspitalg. 6
+43 1 401 700
www.stanna.at

Wiener Privatklinik*
9, Pelikang. 15
+43 1 401 800
www.wpk.at

10th District
Kaiser-Franz-Josef-Spital
10, Kundratstr. 3
+43 1 601 910

Preyersches Kinderspital
pediatric hospital
10, Schrankenbergg. 31
+43 1 601 130

12th District
Unfallkrankenhaus Meidling
trauma center
12, Kundratstr. 37
+43 1 601 500

13th District
Krankenhaus Hietzing
13, Wolkersbergerstr. 1
+43 1 801 100

Orthopädisches Spital Speising*
13, Speisungerstrasse 109
+43 1 801 820

14th District
Hanusch Krankenhaus
14, Heinrich Collin Str. 30
+43 1 910 210

Sozialmedizinisches Zentrum Baumgartner Höhe
psychiatric hospital
14, Baumgartner Höhe 1
+43 1 910 600

16th District
Wilhelminenspital
16, Montleartstr. 37
+43 1 491 500

19th District
Privatklinik Döbling*
19, Heiligenstädter Str. 57-63
+43 1 360 660
www.privatklinik-doebling.at

Rudolphinerhaus*
19, Billrothstr. 78
+43 1 360 360

20th District
Unfallkrankenhaus Lorenz Böhler
trauma center
20, Donaueschingenstr. 13
+43 1 331 100

22nd District
Social Medical Center Ost (SMZ) - Donauspital
22, Langobardenstr. 122
+43 1 288 020

Health Care Glossary

I need an ambulance.	Ich brauche einen Krankenwagen.
My address is . . .	Meine Adresse ist . . .
My name is . . .	Mein Name ist . . .
My telephone number is . . .	Meine Telefonnummer ist . . .
Take off your clothing, please.	Bitte, machen Sie sich frei.
accident	der Unfall
aches and pains	die Schmerzen
acid indigestion	das Sodbrennen
acupuncture	die Akupunktur
after-hours pharmacy service	der Apotheken-Bereitschaftsdienst
all health insurance accepted	alle Kassen
allergy	die Allergie
ambulance	die Rettung
appendicitis	die Blinddarmentzündung
arm	der Arm
aspirin	das Aspirin
asthma	das Asthma
athlete's foot	der Fusspilz
bee sting	der Bienenstich
bleeding	die Blutung
body	der Körper
bone	der Knochen

birth control	die Empfängnisverhütung
blind	sehbehindert
blister	die Blase
burn	die Verbrennung
certificate for foreign care	der Auslandsbetreuungsschein
chest	die Brust
children's clinic	die Kinderklinik
chin	das Kinn
choking	das Ersticken
circumcision	die Beschneidung
cold	die Erkältung
cold sore	der Herpes, die Fieberblasen
condom	das Präservativ, das Kondom
constipation	die Verstopfung
consultation hours	die Ordinationszeiten
contact lens solution	die Kontaktlinsenlösung
corn, callus	das Hühnerauge, die Schwiele
cough	der Husten
cough drops	das Hustenbonbon
cough syrup	der Hustensaft
cuts, scrapes	die Schnittwunden, die Abschürfungen
ear	das Ohr
earache	die Ohrenschmerzen
elbow	der Ellbogen
eye	das Auge

deaf	gehörlos
dentist	der Zahnarzt
dentistry & orthodontics	die Zahn-, Mund- und Kieferheilkunde
deposit	die Einlage
dermatology and venereal diseases	die Haut- und Geschlechtskrankheiten
diarrhea	der Durchfall
disabled parking permit	der Behindertenausweis
disabled parking place	der Behindertenparkplatz
district health boards	die Gesundheitsämter
doctors-on-call	der Ärztefunkdienst
drugstore	die Drogerie
ear, nose and throat doctor	der Hals-, Nasen- und Ohrenarzt (HNO Arzt)
emergency	der Notfall
emergency care	der Notdienst
emergency room, trauma center	das Unfallspital
eye drops	die Augentropfen
fever	das Fieber
fever blisters	das Fieberbläschen
foot	der Fuss
gas	die Blähungen
general hospital	das Allgemeine Krankenhaus

general practitioner	der Allgemeinmediziner, der praktische Arzt
gum soreness	die Zahnfleischschmerzen
gynaecologist	der Frauenarzt, der Facharzt für Frauenheilkunde
gynaecology and obstetrics	die Frauenheilkunde und Geburtshilfe
handicapped	behindert
handicapped accessible	behindertengerecht
hangover	der Kater
hay fever	der Heuschnupfen
head	der Kopf
headache	die Kopfschmerzen
health attack	der Herzanfall
health insurance agency	die Gebietskrankenkasse
health insurance company	die Krankenkassen (KK)
health insurance fund	die Kasse
health treatment voucher	der Krankenschein
heart	das Herz
heart attack	der Herzanfall
heartburn	das Sodbrennen
hemorrhoids	die Hämorriden
hives	das Nesselfieber
hospital	das Krankenhaus

insurance	die Versicherung
internal medicine	die Innere Medizin
itching	das Jucken
jaw	der Kiefer
knee	das Knie
leg	das Bein
loss of consciousness	die Bewusstlosigkeit
medical laboratory	das medizinische Laboratorium
medical referral voucher	der Überweisungsschein
medical specialty	das Fachgebiet
men's health	die Männergesundheit
meningitis	die Hirnhautentzündung
midwife	die Hebamme, die Geburtshelferin
migraine	die Migräne
Mother-Child Passport	der Mutter-Kind Pass
mouth	der Mund
muscle soreness	der Muskelkater
nasal congestion	die verstopfte Nase
nausea	die Übelkeit
neurology and psychiatry	die Neurologie und die Psychiatrie
no health insurance accepted	keine Kassen
nose	die Nase
obstetrician	Facharzt für Geburtshilfe

on-call dentist	die Zahnarztbereitschaft
ophthalmology	die Augenheilkunde
orthopedics and orthopedic surgery	die Orthopädie und orthopädische Chirurgie
outpatient services	die Ambulanz
pediatrician	der Kinderarzt
pediatrics	die Kinder- und Jugendheilkunde
pharmacy	die Apotheke
pharmacy after-hours service	der Apotheken Nacht- und Notdienst
physical therapy	die Krankengymnastik
poison center	die Vergiftungsinformationszentrale (VIZ)
pollen alert service	der Pollenwarndienst
pregnancy test, kit	der Schwangerschaftstest
pregnant	schwanger
prescription delivery service	der Medikamentenzustelldienst
preventive medical check-up	die Vorsorgeuntersuchung
private health insurance	die Privatversicherung
professional license	der Gewerbeschein
psychiatric emergency services	der Sozialpsychiatrische Notdienst
pulmonary disease	die Lungenkrankheit
radiology (x-rays)	die Radiologie, das Röntgen
rash	der Ausschlag

self-insured	selbstversichert
senior citizen	der Pensionist, die Pensionistin
serious accident	der schwere Unfall
severe bleeding	die starke Blutung
severe breathing difficulties	die schwere Atemnot
severe hemorrhage	der schwere Blutsturz
severe pain	die heftigen Schmerzen
shoulder	die Schulter
sinus inflammation	die Nebenhöhlenentzündung
social security	die Sozialversicherung
sore throat	die Halsschmerzen
special care	die Sonderklasse
spermicidal jelly for a diaphragm	das Vaginalgel für das Pessar
stomach	der Magen
sunburn	der Sonnenbrand
surgery	die Chirurgie
TBE immunization	die Zeckenschutzimpfung
Tick-Borne Encephalitis (TBE)	die Frühsommer-Meningoenzephalitis (FSME)
toe	der Zeh
tooth	der Zahn
urologist	der Urologe
urology	die Urologie
vacation voucher	die Urlaubsüberweisung
vaccination	die Impfung

vascular surgery	die Gefässchirurgie
vitamin, multivitamin	die Vitamine, das Multivitaminpräparat
vomiting	das Erbrechen
wheelchair	der Rollstuhl

SAFETY

Photo Credit: Laurie Richardson

11. SAFETY

Good to know . . .

Learn Austria's emergency phone numbers (toll-free):

122 Fire Department (*Feuerwehr*)

133 Police Department (*Polizei*)

144 Ambulance (*Rettung*)

Learn the Europe-wide emergency phone number:

112 European emergency number

When you call this toll-free number from any telephone in any EU country, an operator will connect you to the appropriate service.

Call only in an emergency when you need an immediate response, for example, when a person is in danger of bodily harm or if a crime is in progress. If the situation is not urgent, call your local police station. Dial 059 133 from any phone in Austria to be connected directly to the police precinct nearest to you.

Watch for trams (*Strassenbahnen*) when walking and driving in Vienna. They always have the right of way. Tram tracks cross car lanes, intersections and the middle of some streets.

Fire Department

Vienna has an excellent fire department (*Feuerwehr*) with 26 stations located throughout the city. The main fire station, in the 1st District at Am Hof, has been in the same location since 1592. For a list of fire stations, see: www.wien.gv.at/feuerwehr/organisation/kontakt.

Police

The police (*Polizei*) are present in most neighborhoods throughout Austria. You'll find police stations

(*Polizeiinspektion* or *Polizeidienststelle*) in apartment houses, underground railway stations, next to stores and in many other accessible places. Look for the blue sign with a red stripe and the word *Polizei*. To reach your local police station for non-emergency assistance, call 059 133.

Home Safety

Your home is your castle and you want to keep it, you, your family and your guests safe. Here are a few tips:

- Learn the emergency numbers: 112, 122, 133, and 144. Program them into your telephone.

- Copy the **In Case of Emergency** pages, found at the back of this book, and keep them near your telephone.

- Buy a fire extinguisher and learn how to use it.

- Do not buzz in or open the door for anyone you don't know. Ask for identification.

- If you have the kind of door that can lock you inside, make sure that a key is always accessible.

- Put up smoke alarms, and check them once a month to ensure they work properly.

- Space heaters in winter are popular. If you use one, keep it at least three feet (one meter) away from anything flammable. Never leave it on when you go out.

- An older building may have an old electrical system. Be

careful about overloading electrical outlets.

- Whether you live in an apartment or house, make an evacuation plan for yourself and your family, and rehearse it. This should include a "safe point" where you plan to meet once outside the building.

- Notice the exits in your apartment building. Remember, do not take the elevator in case of a fire.

Pickpockets

Here are a few tips to reduce your chances of becoming a victim:

- Carry only as much cash as you need.

- Carry purses and handbags with the zipper or flap next to your body. Bury your wallet in the bottom of your bag or in a secure pocket.

- Never leave your bag hanging on the back of the chair in a restaurant or cafe, as this provides opportunity for snatching.

- Men should keep their wallets in front pockets. If possible, keep them zipped in an inside jacket pocket.

- Avoid large crowds. If someone pushes you, turn and look at the person's face. If a person feels the threat of being recognized, he or she will be more likely to abandon the attempt to rob you.

- Pay particular attention in crowded areas, for example, in the U-Bahn, S-Bahn and buses at peak times, on escalators, in markets and at large events.

- If you lose your credit card, contact the issuing company immediately and ask them to cancel it.

- Be careful when using your bank card. People usually stand a few steps behind you; be aware of anyone who may be watching over your shoulder.

- Some common techniques that professional pickpockets and purse snatchers use include:

  - A passer-by jostles you on the street or public transportation. While the person apologizes, or during the moment of confusion, the accomplice will pick your pocket or handbag.

  - Someone spills something on you. While the person apologizes or helps you clean it off, he or an accomplice robs you.

  - A pedestrian drops coins on the ground. While you help collect the change, the perpetrator or an accomplice picks your pocket.

Lost and Found

If your important documents, for example, passport, driver's license or car registration, are lost or stolen, file a report at the nearest police station. You will need a police report or loss confirmation to obtain copies or replacement of your documents as well as for insurance purposes. In the case of a lost driver's license or car registration, the police report can serve as temporary proof of entitlement.

Report the loss or theft of other valuables to the nearest Municipal District Office (*Magistratische Bezirksamt*) or the Vienna Lost and Found Office *(Fundamt Wien)*. The Lost and Found Office Web site lets you track your case online.

Vienna Lost and Found Office
Fundamt Wien
www.fundamt.gv.at

If you find or lose something outside the city of Vienna, report it to the local authorities. In addition, you can search for your lost item on the Austrian Lost and Found website: www.fundinfo.at. You may be required to pay a reward to the person who found your item, which can be up to ten percent of the item's value.

Write your telephone number and e-mail address in your passport. If someone turns it in to a consulate or embassy, they will be able to contact you. Inquire at your consulate or embassy to see if your lost item has been turned in.

If you find something, place it in a Lost and Found container located next to a Municipal District Office. However, if the item is an important document, such as a driver's license, passport or vehicle registration, take it to the nearest police station. For items lost or found on public transportation, contact *Wiener Linien*.

Vienna Transportation Authority Lost and Found Service
Fundservice der Wiener Linien
3, Erdbergstrasse 202
+43 1 790 9188
Mon – Wed and Fri 0800 – 1500
Thu 0800 – 1730
funde@wienerlinien.at

ÖBB Lost & Found

For items lost or found on a train or at an ÖBB train station
in Vienna, see: www.oebb.at/en/Services/Lost_and_Found

Subway Safety

The Vienna subway (*U-Bahn*) is safe, even until the last
train around midnight. However, pickpockets are active in
many stations, targeting victims in crowded cars and on
crowded stairways. Pay special attention in these four major
U-Bahn stations: Karlsplatz, Längenfeldgasse, Westbahnhof
and Praterstern. They can be very crowded. Be attentive
and keep your handbags close and closed. The police patrol
regularly, and there is a police office in these stations where
you can go if you need help.

Train Safety

Travel on the Austrian Federal Railway (*ÖBB*) is safe.
Following common-sense guidelines when traveling is
always recommended.

- Never leave your luggage unattended. You can check your baggage on the train, just as you would on an airplane. You can purchase insurance to cover your valuables. A convenient and safe way to handle your luggage is door-to-door service (*Haus-Haus Gepäckservice*). An agent picks up your luggage from your home and delivers it to any address in Austria.

- If you have a small carry-on bag, keep it with you at all times.

- Keep your valuables with you if you nap or sleep. Do not leave valuables in clothing which hangs next to the door or in bags placed on the floor.

- Always lock the door of a sleeping compartment.

- The *ÖBB* has special compartments for women traveling alone. You can book a seat in a women's compartment (*Damenabteilung*) in advance. In general, the train attendant is in close proximity of the compartment.

Auto Safety

- Never leave valuables — wallet, passport, cell phone, car registration papers — in your car.

- Do not leave anything visible inside your car that may attract a thief's attention.

- If your car is equipped with a removable radio, take it out when you leave the car unattended.

- Do not pick up hitchhikers.

- Always lock your car, even in small towns. If something in your unlocked car is stolen and there is no evidence of a break-in, your insurance company may not cover the loss or damages.

- Car theft is prevalent in some countries bordering Austria. If you take your car into these countries, consider using an anti-theft steering wheel locking device.

- Never leave an extra ignition key in the car.

- Before driving a rental car into another country, make sure that your rental contract and insurance cover you there.

- Austria's two major automobile associations offer 24-hour emergency service:

  - ARBÖ
    www.arboe.at

  - ÖAMTC
    www.oeamtc.at

Safety in Parking Garages

Most public parking lots are well-lighted and safe. Many have special parking places near the entrance designated for women only (*Frauen Parkplatz*). Look for the spaces marked with a pink stripe or with flowers on the wall.

Women's Safety

The organizations below counsel and assist women who are victims of violence:

Women Against Violence Europe
WAVE's principal mission is to collect and disseminate data on organizations working in the field of violence against women. You can find information on women's shelters, legal assistance and health care on their website: www.wave-network.org

Women's Helpline
+43 800 222 555
The 24-hour telephone service offers crisis counseling for women, children and teenagers who are affected by violence. You can download a brochure in English from their website: www.frauenhelpline.at

Women's Emergency Line (*Frauennotruf*)
+43 1 717 19
A 24-hour anonymous helpline – a service of the City of Vienna – provides counseling, crisis support and information for women and girls facing physical, sexual or psychological violence: frauennotruf@wien.at

Crisis in Vienna
This helpful guide lists organizations, individuals and centers offering crisis assistance for women, children or families. It is available at the United Nations' Women's Guild (UNWG) Kiosk in the Vienna International Center.

Americans Overseas Domestic Violence Crisis Line

This is an international toll-free domestic violence and child abuse hotline for Americans in foreign countries.

Dial 0800 200 288 to reach the AT&T operator in Austria. Then ask to be connected to 1 866 879 6636. Or contact the hotline by e-mail at:
866uswomen@866uswomen.org (general information)
crisis@866uswomen.org (domestic violence issues)

Discrimination

Austria has an anti-discrimination law (*Gleichbehandlungsgesetz*) which prohibits workplace discrimination on the basis of sex, sexual orientation, ethnic origin, religious belief and age. It is also against the law to deny goods or services to individuals on the basis of ethnic origin.

Discrimination against people with disabilities is prohibited by the Disabled Persons Employment Act (*Behinderteneinstellungsgesetz*) and the Disabled Persons Equal Opportunities Act (*Behindertengleichstellungsgesetz*). Both apply to private and federal employment and contracts governed by federal law.

If you believe you are the target of discrimination, you can file a complaint with the Federal Social Welfare Authorities (*Bundessozialamt*): www.bundessozialamt.gv.at
If you cannot settle the dispute within three months, you can file a lawsuit with the courts.

The US State Department advises American citizens who are victims of crimes overseas to contact the nearest US embassy, consulate, or consular agency for assistance. Citizens of other countries should likewise contact their embassies in case of a crime.

For anti-racism and anti-discrimination resources and organizations in Austria, see the website of the European Network Against Racism: www. enar-eu.org

Traveling Abroad

It is always a good idea to check with your country's consulate before making any trip abroad. The US State Department issues Travel Warnings when it recommends that citizens avoid travel or exercise caution when visiting a specific country. It issues Travel Alerts when it considers that there is a potential of terrorist threat or other relatively short-term and/or trans-national condition that poses significant risks to the security of American travelers. US and other citizens may want to consider the alerts before traveling. To view Warnings and Alerts, go to the State Department travel site: travel.state.gov

Safety Glossary

accident	der Unfall
ambulance	die Rettung
door-to-door delivery service	das Haus-Haus-Gepäckservice
emergency	der Notfall
fire	das Feuer
fire department	die Feuerwehr
lost and found	der Fundservice
municipal district office	das magistratische Bezirksamt
police department	die Polizei
police station	die Polizeiinspektion, die Polizeidienststelle
social services office	das Bundessozialamt
women-only parking space	der Frauen Parkplatz
women's train compartment	das Damenabteil

Pets

Photo Credit: Jerry Barton

12. PETS

Good to know . . .

You can find up to date information regarding pets in Vienna at: www.wien.gv.at/gesellschaft/tiere

Check entry requirements with the Austrian Consulate and your veterinarian before bringing your pet in to the country. For links to pet importation regulations, see: www.wien.gv.at/gesellschaft/tiere/tiergesundheit/reisen/index.html

Get a pet passport: dogs, cats and ferrets must have a passport with vaccination records and an implanted animal identification chip. You can get these from your vet.

Keep Vienna's streets clean by picking up after your dog. Use one of the free black plastic bags located in dispensers throughout the city. You can find a complete list of dispenser locations at: www.wien.gv.at/umwelt/ma48/sauberestadt/hundekotsackerl/index.html

Locate dog areas (*Hundezone*) in your neighborhood where dog owners may let their dogs off the leash. To find a dog zone near where you live, check www.wien.gv.at/stadtplan/en, then click to expand "Art and leisure" and then click "Off-leash dog area" to find a dog zone near you. Also see: www.wien.gv.at/umwelt/parks/hundezonen

Get a muzzle (*Beisskorb*) for your dog if you plan to take your pet on public transportation. Dogs must also be on the leash.

Bringing Pets to Austria

Although Austria does not quarantine dogs or cats, regulations govern the import of animals. Animals on the endangered species list may not be imported; import of birds, turtles, horses, rabbits and fish is strictly controlled. Contact the Austrian Embassy or Consulate in your home country before you move with a pet. A useful website to research requirements is: www.austria.org/pet

Cats and dogs brought into Austria must have an International Vaccination Passport (*Internationale Impfausweis*). You can get the necessary form at the Austrian Embassy or Consulate in your home country. A licensed veterinarian must complete and sign the form. In the US, a representative from the Department of Agriculture must also certify the form. The forms must accompany your pet in transit, and be presented to customs officials.

The vaccination certificate records your pet's most recent rabies (*Tollwut*) vaccination. An animal older than 12 weeks must have the rabies vaccination administered at least 30 days, but no more than one year, before entering Austria. The vaccination certificate includes the pet's breed, age and appearance, as well as the owner's contact information.

Pet Transportation

International pet transportation services arrange for your pets' move to Austria if they are not travelling with you. They provide necessary forms and arrange for local agents to transfer your pets to and from the airport.

Canine Carriers
Arrange transportation for all pets, not only dogs:
www.caninecarriers.com

Dog License

Dog owners in Vienna pay an annual license fee (*Hundesteuer*). You must get a license for your dog within

14 days of arrival, or 14 days after your dog is aged 3 months. You can register your dog at any city cashier (*Stadtkassa*) or online at: www.wien.gv.at/amtshelfer/finanzielles/rechnungswesen/abgaben/hundeabgabe.html

The city will send you a license renewal registration in January with payment due in April.

Taking Dogs Out

In all public areas you must keep your dog on a leash (*Leine*) or put on a muzzle (*Beisskorb*). Your dog may run free in designated off-leash exercise areas. See: www.wien.gv.at/umwelt/parks/hundezonen and look for off-leash dog area (*Hundezone*) or dog run (*Hunde Auslaufplatz*).

The city may fine you if your dog is without a leash and muzzle outside of these areas. If your dog or cat bites a person, the animal must be tested for rabies and you will be subject to a fine or other penalties.

It is against the law to allow your dog to use steps, sidewalks, pedestrian areas, residential streets, sandboxes or children's playgrounds as toilets. You are required to clean up after your pet or be subject to a fine. Dog cleanup bags are available in dispensers around the city and in parks. See: www.wien.gv.at/umwelt/ma48/sauberestadt/hundekotsackerl

Dog Bathing Areas: Donauinsel and Neue Donau

For our four-legged friends, there are two dog exercise areas with water access. The dog beach on the north of the *Donauinsel* between *Floridsdorfer Brücke* and *Nordbrücke* is on the left bank of the Danube. The southern beach is on the left bank of the *Neue Donau* between *Stadlauer Ostbahnbrücke* and the *Praterbrücke*. Both are clearly marked and have dog bag dispensers. Tram 31 will take you to the north beach and U2 or bus 91A goes to the south beach.

No Dogs Allowed

Some parks and public areas do not allow dogs. Look for the sign *Hundeverbot* at the entrance to the park.

Lost and Found Pets

If you find a stray animal, call the Animal Welfare Helpline +43 1 4000 8060 or complete an online form at: www.tierschutzinwien.at/de/Gefunden-und-Verloren

The helpline is open from 0800 to 1800 weekdays and from 0900 to 1500 on Saturdays. If you lose your pet, use the same number.

The Vienna Animal Rescue Service (*Wiener Tierrettung*) +43 1 699 2480 takes lost animals to the animal shelter (*Wiener Tierschutzhaus*) free of charge.

Traveling with Your Pet

Dogs on public transportation must be on a leash and wear a muzzle. You must buy a half-price ticket unless you have a yearly transportation card. You do not need a ticket if you have a small dog in a carrier or a guide dog for the blind. If you travel with your pet outside Austria, you may need additional documents or vaccinations.

Regulations vary for different countries. For requirements, phone +43 1 4000 8060 or e-mail tierschutz@ma60.wien.gv.at or see the website: www.wien.gv.at/english/veterinary/travel

Pet Sitters and Kennels

If you need pet care while you're away, there are kennels and dog and cat sitters in Vienna. Ask your veterinarian to recommend a pet sitter or kennel.

Pet Clubs and Organizations

The Austrian Kennel Club is the umbrella organization for about 100 dog clubs in Austria. The website has links to European dog shows.

Austrian Kennel Club
Österreichischer Kynologen Verband
www.oekv.at

The Friends of Animals (*Tierfreund*) website offers links to organizations and clubs for dogs, cats and other pets as well as zoos and other animal-related organizations: www.tierfreund.at

Vienna Animal Protection Society (*Wiener Tierschutzverein*) www.wr-tierschutzverein.org

Check here for a lost pet or to adopt a new one. The costs are reasonable and the staff knowledgeable. The website includes a list of documents required to take pets to other countries.

Pet Supply Stores

Pet supply shops (*Tierfachgeschäfte*) carry a variety of food, clothes, toys and supplies for all kinds of pets.

Drugstores and grocery stores also sell pet food and supplies. Fressnapf, one of Europe's largest pet supply store chains, has a range of pet foods. Search www.fressnapf.at to find the nearest store.

Veterinarians

You can find a veterinarian on www.tierarzt.at.
Vets can recommend a boarding facility (*Tierpension*) and grooming salon (*Hundesalon*). Most vets speak English.

You must get pet insurance (*Haustierversicherung*) in Austria; ask your insurance agent to include it in your house contents insurance.

To find a vet, you can also see:

University of Vienna School of Veterinary Medicine
www.vetmeduni.ac.at

University of Vienna Small Animal Clinic *Kleintierklinik*
Good for serious injuries or illnesses. English-speaking
staff. Emergency services available 24 hours a day, seven
days a week.

Emergency Vet Services

Most vets offer patients an emergency contact number.
Alternately look for an on-duty emergency vet in your
district: http://www.notruf.at/branchen/tiere

Homeopathic Pet Remedies

Homeopathic treatments are commonly used by Austrian
veterinarians. Many pharmacies carry these remedies.

Pet Burial Service

If your pet dies, you can opt for burial in the pet cemetery
(*Tierfriedhof*): www.tfwien.at or cremation in the
Tierkrematorium: www.wtk.at. If your vet puts the animal to
sleep, you pay for transportation to the crematorium. For
more information see:
www.wien.gv.at/gesellschaft/tiere/tierfriedhof

Pets Glossary

dog license	die Hundesteuer
dog run	der Hundeauslauf
emergency vet service	die Nottierarztvermittlung
handicapped	behindert
International Pet Vaccination Certificate	der internationale Impfausweis
kennel	die Tierpension
leash	die Leine
muzzle	der Beißkorb
No dogs allowed	Hundeverbot
off-leash area	die Hundezone
origin and health certificate	das Ursprungs- und Gesundheitszeugnis
pet	das Haustier
pet ambulance	der Tierrettung
pet burial service	die Tierkörperbeseitigung
pet groomer	der Hundesalon
pet insurance	die Haustierversicherung
pet store	das Zoofachgeschäft
rabies	die Tollwut
veterinarian	der Tierarzt

GROCERIES & GOURMET

Photo Credit: Lenka Peugniez

13. GROCERIES & GOURMET

Good to know . . .

Opening-hours vary, so check at your favorite grocer. Many grocery stores are open from 0700 - 2000. Some smaller neighborhood stores close at noon or 1300 on Saturday. Most grocery stores are closed on Sunday and public holidays.

Bring a coin with you to unlock a supermarket shopping cart. The coin pops out when you return the cart and lock it in place.

Bring your own bags to the grocery store or buy them for a nominal fee. Some stores place produce boxes near the checkout for your use.

Bag your own groceries or do it the Austrian way which is to place your purchases in the cart, move the cart to a side counter, and then pack groceries into bags or boxes.

Large supermarket chains have stores in every neighborhood; most have several. You can also find small grocery shops in many shopping districts.

Supermarkets and Grocery Stores

Billa, Merkur and Spar are the three largest supermarket chains in Vienna. The discount food chains Hofer, Zielpunkt and Penny offer lower prices but offer a more limited selection. Here are the largest supermarkets in Vienna:

- Billa: www.billa.at

- Hofer: www.hofer.at

- Merkur: www.merkurmarkt.at

- Penny: www.penny.at

- Spar: www.spar.at

- Zielpunkt: www.zielpunkt.at

Grocery Service Counters

At grocery service counters, such as the bakery or deli counter, you usually take a number, then wait your turn to order. If you hesitate when it's your turn, another customer will place an order, and you'll have to wait.

Typically, you order such items as rolls, pastries and pork chops by the piece. For example, to order four pork chops, say, "*Vier Schweinskoteletten, bitte.*"

You can ask for a quarter, a half or a whole loaf of bread at the bakery counter.

For sliced meats and cheeses, most people order by the number of slices or by weight. Although most stores price these types of deli items per 100 grams, most people order them in 10-gram portions (*Dekagram* or *Deka* for short).

Bottle Deposit

You pay a deposit (*Pfand*) on many glass beverage bottles. Look for the word *das Pfand* on the bottle. To receive a refund of your deposit, take the empty bottles to a bottle collection machine in any supermarket. The machine scans the bottle and determines the deposit. When you have scanned all of your bottles, press the green button, and the machine prints your receipt (*Flaschenzettel*). Present the receipt at checkout to receive your refund.

Weighing Produce

In most supermarkets, you weigh your produce before you checkout. First note the name or number of the item located on the sign above or below the produce. Then follow these steps:

- Place the item or bag on a scale located in the produce department.
- Press the button that has a picture, name or number corresponding to your item.
- The scale prints a sticker with the weight and price of your item.

Grocery Checkout

Some larger grocery stores have express checkout for customers who purchase ten items or less. If you are not in a hurry, it is customary to let a customer with only a few items go ahead of you.

Stores Open Late and On Sunday

Gas stations often carry packaged foods and drinks including milk. Major transportation hubs like the airport and main train stations have stores with extended opening hours. Currently, the following stores have locations which are open late and some are open on Sundays and holidays:

- Anker Brot: www.anker-brot.at

- Billa: www.billa.at

- Der Mann: www.dermann.at

- Merkur: www.merkurmarkt.at

- OKAY
  Located in Westbahnhof, Südbahnhof, Schottentor and Wien Mitte train stations.

- Ströck: www.stroeck.at

Markets

You can find a wide selection of fresh foods in open-air markets (*Markt*). Located in every district of the city, markets have tables and food booths operated by independent vendors, many of whom are the farmers themselves. Opening hours often change, but these markets are generally open early and closed in the late afternoon or evening. Shop early for the best selection. For more information, including the history of Vienna's markets, see: www.wiener-maerkte.at

You request produce by weight or by quantity. For example, if you want two kilos of apples, say, "*Zwei Kilo Äpfel.* " If you want four apples, say, "*Vier Äpfel.* " The vendor selects the items for you, and asks "Anything else?" (*Alles?* or *Noch etwas?*). If you don't want anything else, say, "*Alles, danke.*"

Naschmarkt

Naschmarkt is the largest outdoor market in Vienna, with stands selling everything from produce and baked goods to Austrian, Turkish and other international specialties. You'll find tropical fruits, fresh meat and seafood, spices, nuts, olives, cheeses, teas, flowers and much more. There are Asian markets, Islamic butchers, several organic booths, cafés and restaurants. There is a large flea market on Saturdays at the Kettenbrückengasse end of the market.

Naschmarkt is located in the 6th District, between the Linke and Rechte Wienzeile and between Getreidemarkt and Kettenbrückengasse. Parking can be difficult. To get there by public transportation, take the U4 to Kettenbrückengasse or Karlsplatz.

City Markets

There are 25 other outdoor markets around Vienna. Hours and days vary. Some are open Monday to Friday; some only on weekends; and others on alternate weeks. In many neighborhoods, there are produce stands and stores that carry fresh produce.

For a complete list of Vienna markets, see: www.wien.gv.at/wirtschaft/marktamt/maerkte

- Brunnenmarkt
  16, Brunneng., Thaliastr. & Yppenplz. 1

- Floridsdorfer Markt
  21, Brünner Str. & Pitkag.

- Genochmarkt
  22, Genochplz. & Erzherzog-Karl-Str.

- Gersthofer Markt
  18, Gersthoferplz.

- Hannovermarkt
  20, Hannoverg. & Othmarg.

- Johann-Nepomuk-Vogl-Markt
  18, Johann-Nepomuk-Vogl-Plz., Kreuzg.

- Kutschkermarkt
  18, Kutschkerg., Gertrudplz.

- Karmelitermarkt
  2, Krummbaumg.

- Meidlinger Markt
  12, Niederhofstr., Rosaliag., Reschg. & Ignazg.

- Meiselmarkt
  15, Hütteldorfer Str. & Johnstr.

- Nussdorfer Markt
  19, Heiligenstädterstr. & Sickenbergg.

- Rochusmarkt
  3, Landstrasser-Hauptstr. & Salmg.

- Schwendermarkt
  15, Schwenderg. & Dadlerg.

- Sonnbergmarkt
  19, Sonnbergplz. & Obkircherg.

- Viktor-Adler-Markt
  10, Viktor-Adler-Plz.

- Volkertmarkt
  2, Volkertplz.

- Vorgartenmarkt
  2, Wohlmutstr. & Ennsg.

Warehouse Stores and Wholesale Market

- Metro
  Membership-only warehouse store, similar to Costco and Sam's Club in the US. See website for locations and membership requirements. www.metro.at

- Grossmarkt Wien-Inzersdorf
  The wholesale market where shop and restaurant owners buy in bulk. There is a flower hall (*Blumenhalle*) that sells flowers in bulk as well as plants. Verify opening hours because this market opens and closes very early and has restricted shopping hours for individuals: www.wien.gv.at/wirtschaft/betriebe/maerkte/grossmarkt/

Gourmet Shops

While supermarkets carry most of your needs, the following stores specialize in gourmet and imported foods:

- Billa Corso: www.billa.at

- Bobby's Foodstore
  Carries British products, including sausages and pastries, and many American foods. The store is open Monday through Saturday and you can also place special orders or shop online: www.bobbys.at

- La Grece: www.lagrece.at

- Meinl am Graben
  Offers gourmet and exotic foods from around the world.

Order online for shipment worldwide:
www.meinlamgraben.at

- Opocensky
  Fine foods and wine from France, Italy and other
  countries. There is a café, catering and a banquet room
  for cocktails, dining or business events:
  www.opocensky.at

Online Shopping

Increasingly, customers are taking advantage of online
shopping and having their groceries delivered. These
companies offer online grocery shopping:

- Billa: www.billa.at

- Hausfreund: www.hausfreund.at

- Merkur: www.merkurdirekt.com

Foods and Beverages

Dairy Products

Dairy products are packaged in smaller quantities than in
other countries. Whole, low-fat, lactose free, soy, almond,
rice and skim milk are available.

You can find milk with an extended shelf life (*Haltbarmilch*)
on the shelf, rather than in the dairy section. It is available in
full- and low-fat. You don't have to refrigerate it until opened,

after which it keeps for four or five days. The date that is stamped on the container is the use-by date.

Meat and Poultry

You can buy pre-packaged and butcher-cut meat in most supermarkets. The butcher (*Fleischhauer*) cuts your order as requested. Keep in mind that pork, beef, veal and lamb cuts may be different from what you're used to.

When you buy meat from a butcher, know what you want ahead of time, or tell the butcher what dish you want to make, and ask him to suggest a cut and quantity of meat.

If language is a problem, write it down, for example, 1½ kilos of roast beef (*eineinhalb Kilo Rostbraten*).

You can order meat by weight, piece or slice, for example, ½ kilo of ground meat (*ein halbes Kilo Faschiertes*), three veal cutlets (*drei Kalbsschnitzel*), or 10 slices of salami (*zehn Scheiben Salami*).

Meat Dishes

A few typical Viennese meat dishes include:

- *Wiener Schnitzel,* a thin slice of veal coated in breadcrumbs and fried. A good Wiener Schnitzel is tender with a light crisp coating.

- *Tafelspitz,* boiled beef Austrian style. A cut of meat served with the broth it was cooked in and accompanied with apple horseradish, sautéed potatoes and creamed spinach.

- *Selchfleisch,* smoked meat served with sauerkraut and dumplings.

- *Rindsuppe,* beef broth.

Baked Goods

Many types of bread (*Brot*) are available in Vienna including heavy white bread (*Sandwich* or *Zeppelin*). Be aware, however, that most bakery breads don't contain preservatives, so buy only what you can eat in a day or two. You can buy half a loaf (*ein Halbes*) of most breads or a quarter of a loaf *(ein Viertel)* of the large round loaves. Favorite breads in Vienna are rye bread (*Roggenbrot*) and Kaiser roll (*Semmel*).

Chain bakeries, including Anker, Ströck, Felber and Der Mann, have freshly-baked breads and pastries throughout the day. Some locations have tables where you can eat a typical Austrian breakfast (*Wiener Frühstück*) of coffee and a roll with butter and jam.

Pastries

It has been said that Vienna is the world capital of pastries. Some well-loved Viennese pastries include:

- *Apfelstrudel,* apples, raisins, nuts and sugar baked in a flaky crust

- *Kaiserschmarrn,* shredded pancakes with raisins, served with fruit compote and powdered sugar

- *Krapfen,* a doughnut, plain or filled with apricot (*Marillen*) or prune (*Powidl*) preserves, or vanilla cream

- *Obsttorte,* sponge cake topped with glazed fruit

- *Sachertorte,* rich chocolate cake with apricot glaze and hard chocolate icing

- *Topfengolatsche,* cheese Danish

- *Vanillekipferl,* small, vanilla-flavored crescent-shaped cookies made with ground almonds or hazelnuts

A bakery (*Bäckerei*) is where you buy breads and bread products. You can usually also buy milk and butter there. A pastry shop (*Konditorei*) does not carry bread but, rather, pastries and sometimes chocolates. A candy maker (*Konfiserie*) specializes in chocolates and candies, and usually does not have pastries or bread. You may find a small area for eating your purchases, or even a full-service café, at all three types of shops.

Here are a few places to enjoy Viennese pastries:

- Aida: www.aida.at

- Demel: www.demel.at

- Konditorei Oberlaa: www.oberlaa-wien.at

- Heiner: www.heiner.co.at

- Sacher Torte Shop: www.sacher.com

Seasonal Foods

Asparagus season (*Spargelzeit*) and mushroom weeks (*Pilzwochen*) are two important times of the year for gourmet food lovers in Austria. In early spring, the appearance of fresh white asparagus is cause for celebration. They're available in abundance and a significant part of many restaurant menus. In the fall, fresh mushrooms appear in the markets, as do game (*Wild*) and pumpkins (*Kurbis*).

Potatoes

You may find varieties of potatoes (*Erdapfel*) in Vienna that are not available in your home country. Here are a few tips for buying and using them:

● *Kipfler,* good for potato salad

● *Sieglinde,* available year round, and good for boiling and potato salad

● *Runde,* good for baking, mashing and making dumplings

Specialty Shops

Asian Food

Asian grocery stores can be found throughout the city, including several at Naschmarkt. Here are a few locations around the city:

- Asia Shop
  22, Wagramerstr. 81
  Donauzentrum
  +43 1 958 9066

- Asiana
  2, Praterstr. 35
  +43 1 922 5212

- Asia Food Center-Mekong
  9, Althanstrasse 29-31
  +43 1 544 2346

- Sino Asia Shop
  4, Rechte Wienzeile 37
  +43 1 585 2347

- Matha Asia Shop
  12, Wilhelmstr. 43
  +43 1 913 9031
  www.matha-asia.com

- Nippon Ya
  4, Faulmanng. 5
  +43 1 586 1084

- Prosi Exotic Supermarket
  7, Wimbergergasse 5
  +43 1 974 4444
  www.prosisupermarket.com

Cake Decorating Supplies

These shops carry everything you need to decorate cakes, including novelty decorations:

- Vienna Dekor Süsswaren
  8, Josefstädterstr. 30
  +43 1 405 6753

- Walter Reimer
  1, Wollzeile 26
  +43 1 512 1433

Halal Food

Hannovermarkt, Brunnenmarkt and Naschmarkt all have Halal shops, or you can try Etsan Supermarkt: www.etsan.at

Ice Cubes

Access to ice cubes (*Eiswürfel*) in Vienna is a challenge if you do not have your own freezer. For daily use, ice cube trays will do, but for parties you need to buy it. Ottakring brewery in the 16th District sells crushed ice and cubes by the kilo. Grocery stores with fish counters, some gas stations, and McDonald's restaurants will sell ice. Or try:

Ottakringer Bier Party Shop
Offers ice, alcoholic and non-alcoholic drinks, snacks and party rentals. www.ottakringershop.at

Wien Eiswürfel
Ice delivery service. www.eiswuerfel.cc

Kosher Food

You can find Kosher foods in larger grocery stores or in specialty shops.

- Butcher Bernat Ainhorn's Shop and Bistro
  2, Grosse Stadgutg. 7
  +43 1 214 5621

- Bäckerei Malkov
  2, Tempelg. 8
  +43 1 214 8394

- Rebenwurzel & Co.
  2, Grosse Mohreng. 19
  +43 1 216 6640

- Supermarket Kosherland
  2, Kleine Sperlg. 6
  +43 1 219 68 86
  www.kosherland.at

- Supermarkt Rafael Malkov
  2, Tempelg. 6/Ferndinandstr. 2
  +43 1 214 8394

Mexican Food

A few sources for Mexican ingredients:

- Casa Mexico
  7, Siebensterng. 16a
  www.casamexico.at

- Oasen Fruchthandels
  6, Naschmarkt Stand 501

- Matha Supermarket: www.matha-asia.com

Organic, Vegan and Health Food

Food products that farmers grow and produce organically and without the use of chemical fertilizers or pesticides are labeled organic (*Bio-Kost* or *Bio: aus biologischer Landwirtschaft*). Austria adheres to European Union regulations on organic foods; some Austrian standards are more stringent.

Many words are the same in English and German, like *Tofu, Seitan, Tempeh, Miso, Tahini, Couscous, Bulgar, Hummus, Vegan(e), Agar-Agar.*

If the label contains these German words, the product contains trans-fats:

- gehärtete Fette verwendet
- können trans-Fettsäuren enthalten
- enthält gehärtete Fette
- pflanzliches Fett, z. T. gehärtet

A comprehensive website on vegan foods in English is: www.happycow.net/europe/austria/vienna

Organic markets (*Biomarkt*) and health food stores (*Reformhäuser*) carry a range of dairy products, meats, foods, juices, produce, diet packages and natural cosmetics. Search *Biomarkt* or *Reformhäuser* for locations. Most supermarkets have a section for organic foods (*Bioecke*).

- Basic
  12, Schönbrunnerstr. 222-228
  +43 1 817 1100 0

- Denn's Biomarkt: www.denns-biomarkt.at

- Natur & Reform: www.natur-reform.org

- Naturprodukte Wallner: www.reformhaus-wallner.at

- Staudigl Reformhaus & Naturparfümerie:www.staudigl.at

- Markt Freyung
  1, Freyung
  Organic farmers sell their products directly to you from May to mid-November on Tues, Wed and Thurs from 1000 – 1830.

- Maran Vegan: www.maranvegan.at

Home Delivery

You can also order organic vegetable and fruit boxes (*Kistl*) online and have them delivered to your home or office.

- Biohof Adamah: www.adamah.at

- Biowichtl Hauszustellung: www.biowichtl.at

Vegan Ingredients

protein	Eiweis
protein from eggs	Eiereiweis
protein from milk	Milcheiweis
salt	Nastrium, Meersalz, Speisesalz
silky tofu	Seiden Tofu
soy milk	Soyamilch
spelt	Dinkel
textured vegetable protein	Sojafleisch, Sojafaschiertes
turmeric	Kurkuma
vegan	Vegan(e)
vegetable broth	Gemusebrühe
vegetarian	vegetarier
vital wheat gluten	Seitan Mehl, Seitan Fix
wafers	Waffeln
whole wheat	Vollkorn
without GMO	ohne Gen

Cooking Measurements Conversions

In most supermarkets and kitchen shops, you can buy a measuring cup (*Messbecher*) with markings for liquid measurements (*Hohlmasse*) in both liters and pints. You can also buy a food scale with readings in ounces or grams.

To convert recipes amounts to metric quantities, see the website: www.metric-conversions.org

Liquid Measurements

US	Metric
8 fluid ounces (fl oz) 1 cup (c)	0.237 liter (l)
16 fl oz 1 pint (pt)	0.473 l
1.06 quart (qt)	1 l
2 pt 1 qt	0.95 l
4 qt 1 gallon (gal)	3.79 l

Dry Measurements

Metric	Metric
1,000 gram (g)	1 kilogram (kg)
1,000 milligrams (mg)	1 kg
1 decagram (dg)	0.1 kg

1 decagram (dag)	10 g
1 hectogram (hg)	100 g

Metric	US
10 g	0.35 oz
15 g	0.53 oz
50 g	1.75 oz
100 g	3.5 oz
250 g	9 oz
500 g	17.5 oz
1,000 g (1 kg)	35.5 oz

US	Metric
1 oz	28.35 g
2 oz	56.7 g
4 oz	113.4 g
6 oz	170.1 g
8 oz	226.8 g
16 oz	453.59 g

Oven Temperature Conversions

° F	° C		
250° F	121° C		
275° F	135° C	Gas mark 1	very slow
300° F	149° C	Gas mark 2	slow
325° F	163° C	Gas mark 2	slow
350° F	177° C	Gas mark 3-4	moderate
375° F	190° C	Gas mark 3-4	moderate
400° F	204° C	Gas mark 5-6	hot
425° F	218° C	Gas mark 5-6	hot
450° F	232° C	Gas mark 7	very hot

Cooking Substitutions

Baking powder (*Backpulver*)	Substitute one 16-gram envelope of baking powder for 1 Tbsp. baking powder
Baking soda (*Natron*)	Substitute one 14-gram envelope of baking soda for 2 Tsp. baking soda
Butter (*Butter*)	Substitute 30 grams for 1 oz (2 Tbsp.) or 113 grams for 4 ounces (8 Tbsp. or 1 stick).
Yeast (*Germ*)	Substitute one 7-gram envelope of dried yeast for ½ cube of fresh yeast (equivalent to 2 Tbsp. + ¼ tsp. dried yeast), enough yeast for 500 g of flour.
Vanilla	Substitute one 8-gram envelope of vanilla sugar (*Vanillezucker*) for 2 Tsp. vanilla or vanilla extract. You can buy liquid vanilla extract at some specialty stores.
Corn syrup	There is no readily available substitute, but you can make your own. To make 1½ cups of corn syrup, dissolve 1 cup sugar in ½ cup water.
Cranberry sauce	Substitute equal amounts of stewed lingonberries (*Preiselbeerkompott*)
Cooking bags	Substitute *Brat-Folie,* sheets of heatproof plastic. Cut to desired length, then tie it at both ends to enclose your food. Cooking bags are available in the aisle with *Folie*.

Caterers

For small parties, the deli counter of your local supermarket can create platters of sliced meats, sausages and cheeses to serve with bread or rolls. For larger functions, especially if you need a banquet room, check with Vienna's hotels. The Vienna Tourism Office offers a brochure about planning a wedding or other large event, including a list of palaces and museums that can be rented. To find a caterer, look online under Catering and Vienna.

Groceries and Gourmet Glossary

You can find most of the words for foods you buy everyday in the dictionary. This Glossary gives you German words that may be harder to find.

bag	das Sackerl
baking powder	das Backpulver
baking soda	das Natron, das Speisesoda
bottle receipt	der Flaschenzettel
bottle deposit	das Pfand
bunch	der Bund
button (on produce scale)	die Taste
chocolate, baking	die Kochschokolade, die Haushaltsschokolade
chocolate, semisweet	die zartbittere Schokolade
condensed milk, sweetened	die gezuckerte Kondensmilch
corn starch	die Maisstärke
cream of tartar	der Weinstein
flour	das Mehl
flour, all-purpose	glattes Mehl, universales Mehl
flour, buckwheat	das Buchweizenmehl
flour, double-sifted	doppelgriffiges Mehl
flour, extra-fine	das Mehl extra-fein
flour, potato	das Kartoffelmehl
flour, sifted	griffiges Mehl

flour, whole-grain	das Vollkornmehl
flour, whole-wheat	das Vollweizenmehl
food coloring	die Lebensmittelfarbe
frozen food	die Tiefkühlkost
health-food store	das Reformhaus
honey	der Honig
horseradish	der Kren, der Meerrettich
lard	das Schweineschmalz
maple syrup	der Ahornsirup
molasses	die Melasse
mushrooms	die Pilze, die Schwammerln
mushrooms, button	die Champignons
mushrooms, chanterelle	die Eierschwammerl, die Pfifferlinge
mushrooms, porcini	die Herrenpilze, die Steinpilze
organic food section	die Bioecke
organic market	der Biomarkt
organic products	die Bioprodukte
pinch (of salt)	die Prise (Salz)
potatoes	die Erdäpfel, die Kartoffeln
potatoes (for baking, mashing)	die Rundekartoffeln (weichkochend)
potatoes (for salad)	die Kipflerkartoffeln
potatoes, new	die Heurigen
potatoes, red	die roten Erdäpfel, die roten Kartoffeln

potatoes, waxy (for boiling)	die Sieglindekartoffeln (hartkochend)
quarter of a...	ein viertel
sale, special offer	die Aktion
sandwich bag	der Jausen-Beutel, der Jausensack
scale (for weighing)	die Waage
tablespoon	der Esslöffel
teaspoon	der Teelöffel
weight	die Gewichte
whole . . .	ein ganzes . . .

Shopping & Style

Photo Credit: Laurie Richardson

14. SHOPPING & STYLE

In this chapter . . .

- Good to know . . .
- Shop Opening Hours
- Where to Find What You Need
- Clothing Sizes
- Shopping Districts and Shopping Malls
- Shopping Excursions Outside Vienna
- Hair Salons
- Beauty Care and Cosmetics
- Second Hand Shops
- Customs Regulations
- Shopping and Style Glossary

Good to know . . .

Austrians say *"Grüss Gott"* to sales clerks
when entering a store, and "*Auf Wiedersehen*" when
leaving. If a clerk asks if you would like help and you are
just looking, tell them, "*Ich schaue nur.*"

The Viennese are stylish dressers and tend to wear
'smart casual' in public. Wearing sweatpants or scruffy jeans
to shops or restaurants is not appreciated. You may receive
better service if you are well dressed.

Clothing sizes are not standard, so sometimes clothing from Italy, France or the UK will be sized according to their system. Don't rely on the marked size for shoes or clothes; try it on first.

Shop Opening Hours

Shopping in Vienna is not 24/7! Standard shopping hours are regulated by Austrian law, and vary from store to store.

Typical opening hours are:

Weekdays 0900 – 1800 or 1900
Some extended hours on Thursday and Friday
Small shops may close at 1300 on Saturday
Sunday Closed

After Hours Shopping

There are some exceptions to the regulated opening hours. When you need something after normal shopping hours, there are a few possibilities:

- Train stations and airports: some groceries available

- Gas stations: many have a small grocery section

Where to Find What You Need

The first thing to figure out when shopping in Vienna is where to find what you need. There are few one-stop shops, so shopping usually requires some planning. Here are some search words that will help you find things:

Looking for . . .	Where to find it	How to say it in German
Books, magazines and newspapers	Book shops, Tabak-Trafik (magazines and newspapers), grocery stores, gas stations. Thalia and Libro carry stationery, school and office supplies	Buchhandlung "Trafik"
Cleaning supplies	Grocery stores, drugstores	Putzmittel
Clothing	Larger stores include Peek & Cloppenburg, C & A, H & M, discounters like Vögele. Palmers specializes in lingerie and hosiery. International brands can be found in shopping malls.	Kleider, Textilwaren
Cosmetics	Drugstore	Drogerie, Parfümerie
Food	Grocery stores, train stations, airports, some gas stations	Lebensmittel

Hardware, DIY, paint, garden materials	Obi, Bauhaus, Baumax, Hornbach, many include garden centers	Baumarkt
Household and kitchen equipment, small appliances	Large grocery stores, large furniture stores, small specialty shops	Haushaltswaren, Eisenwaren
Shoes	Some stock exclusively children's shoes, sports shoes, or comfort shoes	Schuhgeschäft

German Shop	Type of shop	What they sell
Apotheke	Pharmacies	Prescription and OTC medicine and some skin care/ beauty products
Baumarkt	DIY store, builders' supplies	Home improvement materials, garden center, hardware, tools, paint
Drogerie	Drugstore	General health and beauty supplies; health foods, cleaning supplies; photo processing; no prescription medications

Eisenwarenhandlung	Hardware	Hardware, tools, building supplies, garden equipment, cooking utensils
Friseur	Hair Salon	Hair care, hair products, sometimes manicures
Künstlerbedarf	Art supplies	Art and craft materials
Kurzwaren Nähzubehör	Haberdashery, notions	Sewing supplies
Parfümerie	Cosmetics	Makeup and perfume
Reformhaus	Health food shop	Organic foods, beauty and cleaning products
Tabak-Trafik	Newsstand	Newspapers, magazines, cigarettes, tickets for parking and public transport, postage stamps

Clothing Sizes

Proportions may vary and size conversions are approximate.

Women's Sizes

US	6	8	10	12	14	16	18
Austria/Germany	36	38	40	42	44	46	48
Britain	10	12	14	16	18	20	22
France	38	40	42	44	46	48	50
Italy	40	42	44	46	48	50	52

Men's Pants

US	30	32	34	36	38	40	42
Europe	40	42	44	46	48	50	52

Men's Shirts

US	14 ½	15	15 ½	16	16 ½	17	17 ½
Europe	37	38	39	40	41	42	43

Men's Coats and Suits

US	34	36	38	40	42	44	46	48
Europe	44	46	48	50	52	54	56	58

Children's Sizes

US	2	4	6	8	10	12	14	16
Europe	92	104	110/116	128	140	152	164	176

Women's Shoes

US	5	6	7	8	8 ½	9	9 ½
Europe	35	37	38	39	40	41	42

Men's Shoes

US	8 - 8 ½	9 – 9 ½	10 – 10 ½	11 – 11 ½	12 – 12 ½
Europe	41	43	44	45	46

Alterations

Department stores and boutiques will often alter new purchases for a fee. Repair and alteration services for clothing (*Änderungschneiderei*) are found throughout Vienna. The quality of workmanship varies so it is best to ask for a reference from a neighbor.

Shopping Districts and Shopping Malls

Every district in Vienna offers a mix of stores to supply the surrounding neighborhoods with the necessities of life. Neighborhood shops are more easily accessible on foot or by public transportation. If you prefer not to use a car, you may want to invest in a rolling shopping cart to make transporting your purchases easier.

Vienna has a few single-building shopping centers located in the midst of other stores lining major shopping streets. These multi-level air-conditioned spaces are laid out like department stores.

The main shopping malls and shopping areas are shown below. See websites for information on opening hours, locations, and access by public transportation.

District	Shopping Mall	Public Transportation	Website
1st	Kärtnerstrasse, Graben & Kohlmarkt: Vienna's primary tourist and shopping area	U1 Stefansplatz U2 Karlsplatz	www.viennashopping.at/eng/visitors/index.php
1st	Ringstrassen Galerien	U1 Stefansdom U2 Karlsplatz	www.ringstrassen-galerien.at
1st	Steffl Kärtnerstrasse	U1 Stefansdom U2 Karlsplatz	www.kaufhaus-steffl.at
2nd	Stadion Center Next to the Ernst Happel stadium	U2 Stadion Center	www.stadioncenter.at
3rd	Wien Mitte A central transport hub with airport train, new shops	U3 & U4 Landstrasse, Wien Mitte	www.wienmitte-themall.at/en
6th	Generali Center Mariahilferstrasse	U3 Neubaugasse	www.generalicenter.co.at.
6th & 7th	Mariahilferstrasse Vienna's longest shopping street - recently made a pedestrian zone	U2 Museumsquartier U3 Neubaugasse U3 Zieglergasse U3/U6 Westbahnhof	www.mariahilferstrasse.at
7th	Gerngross City Center	U3 Neubaugasse	www. gerngross.at

7th	Spittelberg Known as the furniture district (*Möbelviertel*), includes Spittelberggasse, Breitegasse, Siebensterngasse		
11th	Gasometer Architectural interest - gas tanks from 1899 converted into a shopping, movie theater and apartment complex	U3 Gasometer	www.gasometer.at/ de/einkaufen
11th	Huma Einkaufspark Near Metro shopping warehouse	Bus 73A, 76 A, 79B & 80B	www.huma.at
15th	Bahnhof City Wien West Newly renovated train station open until 2100 weekdays	U3 & U6 Westbahnhof	www.bahnhofcitywie nwest.at/english
15th	Lugner City Stores, restaurants, movie theaters, casino	U6 Burggasse- Stadthalle	www. lugner.at
19th	Q19 Quiet, open & airy	U4 Heiligenstadt Line D Grinzinger Straße	www.q19.at
20th	Millennium City High rise mall	U6 Handelskai (nearby)	www.millennium- city.at

21st	Shopping Center Nord 80 shops & movie theatre	S3 *Schnellbahn* Brünnerstrasse Streetcar 31 & 33 Bus line 431	www.scn.at
22nd	Donauzentrum Near UN and VIS	U1 Kagran	www.donauzentrum. at
Vösendorf	Shopping City Süd (SCS) Europe's largest indoor shopping mall	IKEA operates a shuttle bus from Vienna. See www.ikea.at	www.scs.at

You can find useful resources about Vienna shopping malls on these websites:
www.dovienna.com/shopping/category/malls/
www.vienna4u.at/shoppingmalls.html

Sales

Major sales begin in January and July to make room for merchandise for the following season. However, outlet malls and new marketing concepts with continuous replenishment of stock have made these sales less interesting. Look for bargains when you see these signs:

- *Aktion* – special
- *Saldi* – sale
- *Winterschlussverkauf* – End of winter sale
- *Sommerschlussverkauf* – End of summer sale
- *Totalabverkauf* – Everything must go

Shopping Excursions Outside Vienna

There are major shopping outlets within an hour's drive from Vienna as well as in neighboring countries that offer plenty of opportunity to search for bargains and regional goods.

McArthur Glen Outlet Mall
Offers 170 discounted shops from fashion brands to designer outlets
By car: From Vienna, drive east on the A4 toward Bratislava. Exit at Neusiedl am See - Gewerbepark then follow signs for Outlet Center.
By bus: A shuttle bus runs every Thursday, Friday and Saturday departing across from the Opera (*Staatsoper*) at the entrance on Opernring 3-5, 1010 Vienna. Round trip ticket € 9.50. www.mcarthurglen.at

Freeport
Open seven days a week until 2100. Prices are competitive and there is a supervised kid's area.
By car: Located on the border with the Czech Republic. Drive north out of Vienna to Kleinhaugsdorf, Austria or Znojmo, Czech Republic. www.freeport.cz and

Bratislava, Slovakia
Bratislava, the capital of Slovakia, 70 km from Vienna, is a charming, small city with much to offer the budget-minded shopper, restaurant lover and theater-goer. The major shopping area in Bratislava is "*Obchodna Ulica*". It can be reached by taking Bus 93 from the Main Train Station (*Hlavna Stanica*) to the stop "*Postova*". Both small boutiques and chain stores can be found along this street.

By bus: Buses to Bratislava run from the Vienna Bus Terminal next to Vienna Hauptbahnhof every hour. The trip takes a little more than an hour to Bratislava Bus Station (*Autobusova Stanica*). A round trip ticket costs about €15 which includes transportation for the day on all Bratislava city transportation (buses, trams and trolleybuses). For more information visit: www.slovaklines.sk or www.postbus.at. For information on bus travel within Slovakia, see: www.sadzv.sk

By Train: Trains run to Bratislava Main Station (*Hlavna Stanica*) from Vienna Hauptbahnhof twice an hour. A round trip ticket costs about €17 which includes transportation for the day on all Bratislava public transport. For more information see: www.oebb.at

By Boat on the Danube: The Twin City Liner takes you from Vienna to Bratislava: a very pleasant one hour and fifteen minute trip on the Danube River. Boats depart from the Schiffsstation Wien City at Schwedenplatz (U4) every few hours and cost about €20-30 one way. For more information see: www.ddsg-blue-danube.at

There are two shopping malls near Bratislava:

- **Aupark**
  Reached by Bus 93 from the Bratislava Main Train Station (*Hlavna Stanica*), to the stop "Aupark". www.aupark.sk

- **Avion**
  Near the Bratislava Airport, reached by Bus 61 from the Main Train Station (*Hlavna Stanica*) to the stop "Avion" or "Avion-Ikea". www.avion.sk

Hair Salons

Leaving your favorite hair stylist can be one of the most difficult parts of an international relocation. Whether high-end or cut 'n go, Vienna has a range of hair care salons *(Friseur)* starting from approximately € 50 (for wash, cut, and blow dry) up to about €120.

The main places to find a new stylist are:

* Your neighborhood – search *"Friseur"* plus your postal code

* Shopping malls have chain salons, good for children's hair

* Hotels

Appointments at hair and beauty salons are not always necessary during the week, however weekends and the Ball season (January and February) tend to be busy.

Tipping Your Stylist

Generally, you give a 10% tip to your hairstylist. If a trainee washes your hair, tip €1 - €2. Do not tip the owner.

Hair Salon Vocabulary

English	German	English	German
bangs	Stirnfransen	gel	Gel
bleach	bleichen	hair spray	Haarspray
blow dry	föhnen	hair removal	harzen
bob	Bob	manicure	Handflege
body only	Stützwelle	mousse	Schaum, Mousse
brush	bürsten	pedicure	Fusspflege
color	färben	rollers	Lockenwickler
comb	kammen	set	legen
comb out	auskämmen	setting lotion	Haarfestiger
conditioner	Kurspülung	shampoo	Shampoo
curl	Locken machen	dry hair	trockenes Haar
curling iron	Lockenschere	normal hair	normales Haar
curly	Lockig	oily hair	fettiges Haar
cut	schneiden	dandruff	Schuppen
electrolysis	Epilieren	tease	toupieren
eyebrow plucking	Augenbrau zupfen	trim	Trim
eyelash colour	Wimpen färben	wash	waschen
facial	Gesichtsbehand-lung		

Beauty Care and Cosmetics

Beauty Salons

The beauty industry is booming in Vienna and you'll find salons and cosmeticians offering massages, permanent makeup, manicures and pedicures, hair removal, styling, skin treatment and facials.

There are salons throughout the city, particularly in major shopping areas. Search for *Kosmetikinstitut*. Prices vary and can be high, so it is best to ask when you book the service.

Cosmetics and Skin Care

Finding your favorite brand or product might take some exploring, although most major international brands are available in Vienna. Drugstores *(Drogerie)* carry everyday brands and hypoallergenic make-up *(hypoallergenisches Makeup)*. Cosmetics stores *(Parfümerie)* and some department stores carry high-end brands.

Beauty Care Vocabulary

English	German	English	German
astringent	*Astringierend*	hypoaller-genic	*hypoallergenic*
blush	*Rouge*	lip liner	*Konturenstift*
combination skin	*Mischhaut*	lipstick	*Lippenstift*
deodorant	*Deodorant or Deo*	moisturizer	*Feuchtigkeits-creme*

dry skin	trockene Haut	nail polish	Nagellack
eyeliner	Eyeliner	nail polish remover	Nagellack-entferner
eye-makeup remover	Augen-makeup Entferner	oily skin	fette Haut
face mask	Gesichsts-maske	sensitive skin	empfindliche Haut
facial scrub	Gesichsts-reinigung	trans-luscent powder	transluscent Puder
fragrance-free	geruchlos	waterproof	wasserdicht

Second Hand Shops

Vienna is a great place for second-hand and consignment shopping, Thrift stores are clean, well-organized, and attract all kinds of shoppers.

Charity Shops

- Caritas has two main shops: www.carla-wien.at/carla-laeden/

- Humana has ten locations around Vienna with a wide selection of clothing and accessories for the whole family: www.humana.at

- Christ Church Shop
  Clothing, accessories, books, toys, china, glassware and more: www.christchurchvienna.at/?q=shop

Shops for Profit

For information on second-hand shopping, see: www.wien.info/en/lifestyle-scene/trendy/vintage-vienna-second-hand-fashion

Consignment stores are also popular for formal or vintage clothing, ball gowns and traditional Austrian clothing (*Trachten*) in particular. The turnover in ball clothing and accessories is high and great bargains can be found.

Customs Regulations

Customs (*Zoll*) can inspect any goods you bring into Austria from other countries. Depending on the product and the goods you purchased, import limitation may be a general monetary limit or a quantity limit for a product category. There are restrictions and prohibitions on ivory, exotic leather goods, plants and flower bulbs. You can bring medications for personal use in quantities needed during travel.

Customs regulations vary depending on your departure and transit countries. There are no border controls between nations within the Schengen Agreement, which includes most EU countries. The free customs limits apply to one calendar day per person.

The Finance Ministry (*Bundesministerium für Finanzen*) publishes a booklet called *Customs Info Tips for Foreign Travelers*. Information in English is on the Ministry's website: https://english.bmf.gv.at/customs/travellers/Travellers1.html

Tax-free Imports within the EU

Guidelines change but, in general, the EU permits the import of moderate amounts of most products for personal use. You must have paid taxes on them in the country of purchase and transport them personally. You are not allowed to share total customs-free limits with other passengers. Regardless of the mode of transportation, you can currently bring the following items duty-free into Austria from any EU country:

- Tobacco:
  800 cigarettes, 200 cigars, 1 kilogram tobacco

- Alcohol:
  10 liters spirits, 90 liters wine (60 liters sparkling wine), 110 liters beer

Non-EU Duty-free

The limits for bringing duty-free tobacco products into Austria from a non-EU country are the same as those for an EU country, provided they are for your own use and you transport them personally. However you can bring only a few liters of alcoholic beverages into Austria from non-EU states. You must declare gifts exceeding €175.

Tax-free Goods

Non-Austrian residents traveling directly to a non-EU country can receive a refund of the value added tax (VAT) on purchases exceeding €75 made at any one store in one day. Look for the Tax-Free sign in shop windows. To get your refund, have a store clerk complete and stamp a tax-refund form, then present it, along with your original receipts and the goods you purchased, to the customs officer at the airport or train station when you leave Austria. A customs official must stamp the form for it to be valid. When complete, mail the form to the Austrian tax-free organization. Alternatively, for a fee, some agents will refund the tax in cash as you leave the country. If you are going to Switzerland, expect to pay Swiss VAT tax when you enter the country.

For more information, see: www.wien.info/en/shopping-wining-dining/shopping/tax-free

Shopping and Style Glossary

Do I need batteries to operate this?	Brauche ich dazu Batterien?
Do you accept credit cards?	Nehmen Sie Kreditkarten?
Do you deliver?	Bieten Sie die Zustellung an?
Do you offer assembly?	Bieten Sie den Aufbau an?
Do you offer installation?	Bieten Sie die Installation an?
Do you offer repair services?	Haben Sie einen Kundendienst?
How do I clean this?	Wie kann man das reinigen?
How much does this cost?	Wieviel kostet das?
I'm just looking.	Ich schaue nur.
May I have a receipt?	Könnte ich eine Quittung haben?
What is the fee for this service?	Was kostet dieser Service?
When can I expect delivery?	Wann erfolgt die Zustellung?
Where can I find . . .?	Wo kann ich . . . finden?
Austrian boiled wool fabric	der Loden
Austrian dress	das Dirndl
Austrian traditional dress	die Trachtenkleidung
closeout	der Schlussverkauf
customs	der Zoll

day spa	das Kosmetikinstitut
dry cleaner	die Putzerei
fur coat	der Pelzmantel
furrier	der Kürschner
gloves	die Handschuhe
hair salon	der Friseur
hat	der Hut
leather pants	die Lederhose
laundry	die Wäscherei
neck size	die Halsweite
orthopaedic shoes	die orthopädischen Schuhe
pedicure	die Fusspflege
sale	der Saldi, der Ausverkauf
shoe	der Schuh
shoemaker	der Schuhmacher, der Schuster
tailor shop	die Änderungsschneiderei
tails	der Frack
total sell-out	der Totalabverkauf
tuxedo	der Smoking
winter close-out sale	der Winterschlussverkauf

SOCIAL NETWORKS

Photo Credit: Wendy Williams

15. SOCIAL NETWORKS

In this chapter . . .

- Good to know . . .
- AWA Vienna
- Associated Women's Organizations
- Other Organizations
- School Volunteer Opportunities
- Support Groups

Good to know . . .

Get involved with community organizations to give you a sense of belonging and help ease your transition.

Do your research on the many organizations in Vienna. Attend one or two meetings of those that sound interesting.

Share your skills and make an impact. If you don't find an organization that offers what you want, offer to create a group within an existing organization such as AWA. It's a great way to meet people who share your interest.

Improve your resume by volunteering with an organization. If you are not working full-time, you can develop or learn skills that will be valuable for the future.

Don't let language get in the way. Joining groups or taking classes offers the chance to share an interest that transcends the language barrier. If you're with German speakers, you may improve your language skills too.

The American Women's Association of Vienna (AWA)

AWA Vienna is a non-profit organization founded in 1924 to enable women to broaden their horizons, befriend one another and enhance their understanding of their host country. English-speaking women of all nationalities are welcome to join. Currently the AWA has members from more than 40 countries. It is a dynamic group offering the possibility to do something useful and have fun while making new friends.

The AWA Vienna office is located in the heart of Vienna near Stephansplatz. There is a lending library of English-language books, and internet access for members.

> AWA Vienna
> 1, Singerstrasse 4/11
> +43 1 966 29 25
> awa@awavienna.com

AWA Member Benefits

Members receive a monthly magazine, *Highlights*, and are welcome to use AWA facilities and participate in activities and excursions. Regular events include:

- book club
- girls' night out
- hobby groups
- language classes
- monthly meetings
- social events with partners
- trips and tours
- weekly coffees

The AWA, a member of the Federation of American Women's Clubs Overseas (FAWCO), raises funds and donates goods to community and charitable organizations and also contributes to FAWCO charitable initiatives.

Monthly General Meetings

The AWA holds monthly General Meetings throughout Vienna. Speakers include government officials, journalists, historians, musicians, and travel industry and wine experts. General Meetings also give members a chance to meet one another and sign up for tours and events.

Everybody's Coffee

Every Wednesday morning the AWA hosts a coffee for all members, newcomers to Vienna, and women interested in learning more about our programs. Coffees take place at Café Heiner, at 1010, Kärntnerstr. 21 from 1000 – noon.

Tours and Cultural Events

The AWA organizes tours and cultural events for members and their families. The trips include visits to destinations in Austria and Europe, shopping trips, guided tours to museums, art galleries and other points of interest. The AWA occasionally teams up with the United Nations Women's Guild.

Charity Fundraising

The AWA raises funds for various charitable organizations through an annual holiday bazaar, musical evenings and special fundraising events. The AWA also donates goods in kind to refugees and underprivileged children and takes part in FAWCO charity work.

Highlights

The AWA publishes the magazine *Highlights* ten times per year (no issue July and August). Members receive it in the mail and can consult it online. It is packed with club activities, topical articles, and community events. AWA volunteers publish and distribute *Highlights* and advertising sales offset printing and mailing costs.

Associated Women's Organizations

The AWA has close ties to these groups.

FAWCO
The Federation of American Women's Clubs Overseas
The American Women's Association of Vienna is a member of FAWCO, an international network of over 60 independent women's organizations with a combined membership of over 12,000 women in 35 countries worldwide. www.fawco.org and www.fawcofoundation.org

United Nations Women's Guild of Vienna (UNWG)
Founded in 1967, the UNWG is an international women's organization with 500 members from over 100 different countries. Meetings and activities are open to women with a valid UN grounds pass. Membership is limited to women associated with embassies and the UN.
www.iaea.org/unwg

Daughters of the American Revolution (DAR)
The DAR is a worldwide service organization devoted to promoting historic preservation, education and patriotism. Membership is open to women who can trace their ancestry to a revolutionary war patriot.
www.dar.org and dar.arh-19.at

Vienna Babies Club
The Vienna Babies Club is an independent, non-profit support network for new and expectant expat women living in and around Vienna. Many members have given birth in Vienna and have recommendations for doctors and hospitals, and can give advice on pregnancy, delivery, breastfeeding, and baby-related topics.
www.viennababiesclub.com

Women's Career Network
The Women's Career Network serves as a resource and support network for women seeking to develop and expand their career opportunities.
www.wcnvienna.org

Other Organizations

Here are other organizations that might interest you:

- **Afro-Asian Institute**
  Sponsors cultural exchanges and educational programs:
  www.aai-wien.at

- **African Women's Organization**
  Works with other non-governmental organizations
  involved in the welfare of women and immigrants:
  www.african-women.org

- **agpro**
  A network for gay professionals in Austria: www.agpro.at

- **Austrian-Australian Society** www.australia-austria.at

- **Austro-American Society** www.oag.mov.at

- **Austro-American Institute of Education**
  Promotes cultural interaction between the US and
  Austria: www.aaie.at

- **Austro-Irish Society** www.austro-irish.at

- **Euro-Asian International Fine Art Society**
  Promotes artists from different ethnic and cultural
  backgrounds: www.euroasian.at

- **Friends of South Africa** www.fosa.at

- **L'Amicale des Femmes Francophones**
  Welcomes French-speaking women of any nationality:
  www.amicale-femmes-francophones-autriche.org

- **British Community Association of Vienna**
  www.bca-vienna.com

- **Bruno Kreisky Forum**
  Invites internationally-recognized politicians, business
  people and academics to participate in discussions,
  lectures and seminars: www.kreisky-forum.org

- **Centre International Universitaire**
  Focal point of international student activity in Vienna as
  well as a center for information on academic programs
  and scholarships: www.ciu.at/main.html

- **Democrats Abroad Austria**
  www.democratsabroad.org/group/austria

- **HOSI Wien**
  Homosexuelle Initiative Wien. Combats discrimination
  and fights for equality: www.hosiwien.at

- **Ich bin OK**
  Integrates people with disabilities into theater, dance and
  other modes of expression: www.ichbinok.at

- **Jewish Welcome Service Vienna**
  Provides services for the Jewish community in Vienna:
  www.jewish-welcome.at

- **Labyrinth**
Organizes public readings and literature festivals in English: www.labyrinthpoetry.info

- **Lions Club International**
The Vienna branch of one of the largest and most successful service organizations in the world: www.lions.at

- **Maple Leaf International Business Club**
A private non-profit club that promotes communication and knowledge exchange between the local and international community: www.ml-ibc.com

- **National Council of Women Austria**
Bund Österreichischer Frauenvereine
A non-partisan, non-denominational umbrella organization of Austrian women's organizations: www.ncwaustria.org

- **Ozcon**
The Australian Connection www.ozcon.at

- **Republicans Abroad**
There is no local chapter, but RA Germany serves the needs of Republicans in Austria: www.republicansabroad.de

- **Rosa Lila Villa**
Lesbian and gay center that offers counseling and educates the community: www.villa.at

- **Teachers of English in Austria** www.tea4teachers.org

- **US Chamber of Commerce**
  Promotes economic and trade relations between Austria and the US: www.amcham.at

- **Vienna Lit**
  Holds book discussions and sponsors literary events in English: www.viennalit.at

- **Vienna Toastmasters**
  Helps develop better listening and speaking skills in an environment of team spirit and fun: www.toastmasters.at

School Volunteer Opportunities

The following English language schools welcome volunteers to help in the library, in remedial reading and athletic programs and with special activities:

- **American International School** (AIS) www.ais.at

- **Danube International School** (DIS)
  www.danubeschool.com

- **International Christian School of Vienna** (ICSV)
  www.icsv.at

- **Vienna International School** (VIS) www.vis.ac.at

Support Groups

- **Alcoholics Anonymous**
  www.aa-europe.net/countries/austria.htm

- **Aids Help Center**
  Provides free counseling, advice and support on AIDS-related issues, and confidential HIV testing: www.aids.at

- **BIZEPS Center for Independent Living**
  BIZEPS - Zentrum für Selbstbestimmtes Leben
  A support group for independent living, run by and for people with disabilities, with a multilingual staff:
  www.bizeps.or.at

- **Center for Drug Dependency** www.pass.at

- **Overeaters Anonymous** www.overeatersanonymous.at

FAITH COMMUNITY

Photo Credit: Laurie Richardson

16. FAITH COMMUNITY

Good to know . . .

Freedom of religion is guaranteed by the Austrian government. The independence of legally recognized churches and religious communities is guaranteed in Article 15 of the Federal Constitution. According to Austrian law, any person over age 14 can choose their religion.

Austria has many public holidays related to the Catholic Church calendar. For information see: www.wien.gv.at/menschen/integration/kalender

Grüss Gott! **is a greeting** used in Austria and southern Germany. It literally means "Greeting of God" but for most, it has lost its religious meaning and is used like "Hello" or "Good day."

You can find congregations of most of the world's major religions in Vienna, including Catholic and Protestant churches, Islamic mosques, Jewish synagogues, a Hindu temple and a Buddhist society. For information see: www.wien.gv.at/english/culturehistory/religion/churches.html

The Long Night of Churches (*Lange Nacht der Kirchen*) is an annual event in Vienna. Churches open their doors to the general public to allow them to experience the richness of these sacred places and the diversity of religions in Vienna. For more information see: www.langenachtderkirchen.at

Mass is celebrated with a choir and orchestra in the *Jesuitenkirche* and *Augustinerkirche*, both in the 1st District. The Vienna Boys Choir sings a classical Mass in the *Hofkapelle* at the *Hofburg* most Sundays. For more information about liturgical music see: www.wien.info/en/vienna-for/religious-services

Religions in Vienna

According to government statistics (2008), the religious affiliation of residents registered in Vienna is:

- Roman Catholic 49%
- Muslim 8%

- Orthodox 7%
- Protestant 7%
- Jewish 1%

When you declare a religious affiliation on your residence registration (*Meldezettel*), the government will set a church tax which supports church operations.

Religious education in Austrian schools covers all legally recognized religions. Children who belong to other churches and religious communities may receive the religious education of their choice. The Austrian government pays religious education teachers.

Religious Communities

Buddhist

- www.buddhismus-austria.at/English-Info

Christian

- Calvary Chapel: www.calvarywien.com

- Christ Church Anglican/Episcopal: www.christchurchvienna.org

- Christian Non-denominational International Chapel of Vienna: www.viennachapel.org

- Church of the Latter Day Saints: www.kirche-jesu-christi.at

- Christliche Internationale Gemeinde: www.cigwien.at

- Church of the Seventh Day Adventist: www.vienna-international.adventisten.at

- Crossways International Bible Church: www.crossway.at

- Evangelical Church: www.evang.at

- Four Corners Christian Fellowship: www.fourcorners.at

- Grace Church: www.gracechurch.at

- International Baptist Church: www.ibcv.at

- New City Wien: www.newcitywien.at

- St. Stephen's Cathedral: www.stephanskirche.at

- United Methodist Church: www.esumc.at

- Vienna Community Church: www.viennacommunitychurch.com

- Vienna English-Speaking Catholic Community: www.vescc.org

- Vienna International Religious Center (VIRC): The VIRC, sponsored by the Vienna Roman Catholic Tourist Chaplaincy, provides information on Christian church activities. www.virc.at

- Votivkirche: www.votivkirche.at

- Vienna Christian Center: www.viennachristiancenter.at

- Vineyard: www.vineyard-wien.at/

Hindu

- Hindu Mandir: www.mandir.at

Islam

- Islamic Center: www.izwien.at

- Islamic Community in Austria: www.derislam.at

Judaism

- Information about the rich history and activities of the Jewish community in Vienna: www.wien.info/media/files/jewish-vienna.pdf

- City Synagogue: www.ikg-wien.at

- Or Chadash: www.orchadasch.at

Cemeteries

For history buffs, music and theater fans, bird lovers and anyone who has ever traced a family tree, Vienna's cemeteries and crypts are a source of fascination. A visit to a landscaped, historic cemetery (*Friedhof*) is an encounter with Vienna's soul. The city is famous for its Baroque interest in the details of death and interment. On All Saints

Day, November 1, family and friends place flowers and candles on the graves.

Zentralfriedhof

The 590-acre Zentralfriedhof, Vienna's largest cemetery and one of the largest in the world, has an *art nouveau* church at its center. Many prominent Austrians have their final resting place here. www.friedhoefewien.at

St. Marx Friedhof

The attraction of St. Marx Cemetery is the much-visited probable site of the communal anonymous grave where Wolfgang Amadeus Mozart was buried. The flowering lilac bushes in the spring and worn gravestones of those buried when the cemetery was actively used (1784 - 1874) make for a quiet, meditative visit. www.wien.gv.at/umwelt/parks/anlagen/friedhof-st-marx.html

Imperial Crypt (*Kaisergruft bei den Kapuziner*)

Elaborately sculpted metal sarcophagi hold the bodies of Habsburg family members; their preserved hearts are in the *Augustinerkirche* and their embalmed entrails are in St. Stephen's catacombs. www.kaisergruft.at

Faith Community Glossary

Bible	die Bibel
Bible class	die Bibelstunde
boys' choir	der Knabenchor
choir	der Chor
church	die Kirche
confession	die Beichte
faith	der Glaube
freedom of worship	die Religionsfreiheit
God	der Gott
holy	heilig
Holy Spirit	der Heilige Geist
Koran	der Koran
mass	die Messe
mosque	die Moschee
New Testament	das Neue Testament
Old Testament	das Alte Testament
religion	die Religion
religious affiliation	die Religionszugehörigkeit
religious denomination	die Konfession
religious service, worship	der Gottesdienst
synagogue	die Synagoge
temple	der Tempel
to worship	eine Religion ausüben

Sports & Recreation

Photo Credit: Jerry Barton

17. SPORTS & RECREATION

Good to know . . .

This chapter will help get you started finding places to play your favorite sports. We include links to many organizations, clubs and facilities that are popular with members of AWA Vienna. It is not an exhaustive list of every sport. If your favorite sport is not included, you can find resources on the city's websites, including: www.wien.info/en/vienna-for/sports

To find a fitness center in Austria, look for links to sports clubs (*Sportvereine*) and federations (*Sportverbände*) on www.wien.gv.at/freizeit/sportamt. The site includes an alphabetical listing of sports, with links to hundreds of sports organizations.

Austrian sports organizations websites:

Austrian Sports Federation
(*Österreichische Bundes-Sportorganisation*)
Represents Austrian sports associations and sports clubs: www.bso.or.at/en/home

Austrian Sports Union (*Sportunion Österreich*)
Offers classes and promotes competitive and recreational sport activities: www.sportunion.at

Get free information about sports facilities in Vienna at the City Information Center in the town hall (*Rathaus*) on Friedrich-Schmidt-Platz.

Bicycling

Bicycling (*Radfahren*) is a popular form of recreation and transportation in Vienna. Buying a new bicycle can cost as little as €200. If you plan on touring, expect to spend €600 or more. Retail sporting goods stores sell a wide range of bikes and there are many specialized bike shops in Vienna. It is a good idea to test several bikes, and even rent a few times, before deciding what best suits your needs. If you buy an expensive bike, buy a good lock and store it in a secure place. Bicycle theft is common, even in apartment building storage rooms. You must have wheel reflectors and a bell on your bike if you ride in Vienna. Helmets are not required, but recommended. For information on using City Bikes to travel within Vienna, see the **Transportation** chapter.

Bicycle Repairs (*Service und Reparatur von Fahrrädern*) www.reparaturnetzwerk.at

Some neighborhood shops will only repair or service bikes they have sold. If you bring a bike to Vienna, these shops, among others, offer repairs:

- Cooperative Fahrrad
  Sells touring bikes, and offers fitting, advice and service.
  www.fahrrad.co.at

- Mechaniker Brunner
  16, Degengasse 37
  +43 1 485 5732

- Do-It-Yourself Bike Workshop (*Fahrrad Selbsthilfe Werkstatt*) A non-profit open workshop for people who want to repair and service their bicycles. Advice is available from volunteers and you can borrow some specialized tools. Used parts are available for purchase. www.fahrrad.wuk.at

Bicycle Tours

With over 1,000 miles of bike paths and routes within the city, you can visit all sights effortlessly and quickly. You can find bike maps at most bike shops. Take a look at the route before heading out as some paths are intended for mountain bikes and others have challenging hills. There are many good asphalt bike paths in Austria.

Many Austrian trains will accommodate your bicycle however you do need to buy a ticket for it. Sometimes the Austrian National Railroad (*ÖBB*) requires you to use their From-House-to-House pick-up and delivery service for your bicycle. Even if it's not required, this may be a good idea, especially if your trip requires several train changes. To plan your trip, consult **www.oebb.at** or a travel planner at a train station.

There are several popular bike tours from Vienna. One is to Neuseidlersee. Trains leave at least hourly from the main station (Hauptbahnhof). Paths around the lake are flat, well-marked, and run through sunflower fields, vineyards, orchards and small towns. Another popular bike trip departs from Franz Josefs Bahnhof to Melk. Tour the Melk Abby, then cycle along the Danube to Krems, about 24 miles (40 kilometers), and take the train back from Krems to Hütteldorf.

Bicycle Rentals

You can rent good quality bikes (*Radverleih*) at several locations around Vienna. Prices range from about €1 to €6 per hour or €8 to €36 per 24 hour period. Bring a photo ID to leave behind while you have the rental bike. A few shops rent bikes for touring and can organize delivery and pickup.

Check out these websites:

- www.danube-cycle-path.com/austria-bike-rentals.html

- www.wien.info/en/vienna-for/sports/cycling/bicycle-rentals

- www.wien.gv.at/english/transportation-urbanplanning/cycling

- Nextbike
  You can find Nextbikes at the main train stations, pedestrian zones and other vibrant spots in the city which can be returned to any Nextbike station in Austria. Cost is €1 per hour or €8 per 24 hours. View the website for more details and maps: www.nextbike.at

- Pedal Power
  Rents high quality bikes with locks and arranges bike tours of Vienna. Good tour materials in many languages are available: www.pedalpower.at

- Radsport Nussdorf
  This shop also offers bike repairs: www.donau-fritzi.at

- Copa Kagrana
  Rents bicycles for two or four people for €12 per hour. Also offers rentals for persons with disabilities, and repairs bicycles: www.fahrradverleih.at

Mountain Biking
(*Rundumwien*)
The area of the Vienna Woods that borders the city is ideal for mountain biking. For more information see: www.wien.at/verkehr/radfahren/mtbiking

Inline Skating

You can use Vienna's bike paths for inline skating. Paths along the Danube, 21 km on the Donauinsel, Donaukanal and Prater Hauptallee are very popular. From May to September, inline skaters get together ever Friday evening at Heldenplatz at 2100. You can rent inline skates at the U1 Donauinsel and U6 Floridsdorf stations. For more information see:

- Austrian Skate & Inline Skating Association
  Österreichischer Rollsport & Inline Skate Verband (ÖRSV) www.oersv.or.at

- Skatelab
  2, Engerthstrasse 160-178
  Has mini-ramps, pyramids, fun boxes, quarter-pipes, curbs, rails, etc.

- Friday Night Skating Vienna
  Skate on Vienna's streets (closed to car traffic for the events) every Friday night from May to September, starting at 2100. Consult the website for upcoming routes. Bicyclists are also welcome.
  www.wien.gruene.at/skater

Gyms and Fitness Centers

Joining a gym or fitness club is an economical way to exercise and to meet Austrians. If you have an intermediate understanding of German, you should be able to follow along. Classes are also held in the late afternoon or evening at schools in most districts. There are also courses by age groups for children, for mothers and children, for over-50s and for singles. Some schools offer volleyball and basketball. Some hotels offer gym memberships. Sports clubs offer tennis courts, squash courts and swimming pools. For more information see: www.fitness-center.at

For fitness classes designed for women only, often with babysitting available, see Fitness for Women (*Frau & Sport*):
www.wien.at/freizeit/sportamt/kurse-veranstaltungen/frau

Below are a few of the many gyms and fitness centers in Vienna:

* Beers Vienna Health Club (1st District) www.beers.at

* Fitnessclub Heimlich (3rd District) www.fitnessclub-heimlich.at

* Holmes Place (4 clubs in Vienna) www.holmesplace.at

* John Harris Fitness Center
  Locations in 1st, 2nd and 5th Districts and a medical spa in the 1st District: www.johnharris.at

* Manhattan Sports Clubs www.manhattan.at

Pilates

Below are a few of the many Pilates studios in Vienna:

* Move On Dance Center and Pilates Studio www.moveon.at

- Studio Gabriella Cimino www.pilatescentervienna.com

- Studio 18 Pilates and Yoga   www.pilates-yoga.at

Yoga

For an overview of yoga studios in Vienna, see:
www.yogaguide.at

- BYoga www.byoga.at

- Sivananda Yoga Zentrum
  Has a Yoga shop where you can purchase yoga apparel
  and books. www.sivananda.org/vienna

- Yoga in Daily Life
  Locations in 3rd, 4th and 21st Districts
  www.yoga-im-taeglichen-leben.at

- Yogazentrum Ganesha www.ashtanga.at

- Ashtangavienna Yogazentrum www.ashtangayoga.at

- Yoga & More www.yoganotion.at/

Golf

Golf is very popular in Austria. You can take low-cost short
courses at three clubs within 30 minutes of Vienna. English
instruction is readily available. Many places offer a variety of
membership packages making it easy to try the game with
borrowed equipment and group lessons.

> Austrian Golf Association
> *Österreichischer Golfverband*
> www.golf.at

For a list of all golf courses in Austria, *Golf in Österreich* is available at most pro shops or visit the above website. To be eligible to play on regular golf courses or in tournaments, you must produce your current handicap card. Beginners must attend classes to learn the game and golf etiquette. After you receive a course certificate (*Platzreife*), you are allowed to play on a golf course. You may want to join the GC2000 Club, which allows you to play at clubs all over Austria and offers range fee-free training on most partner systems as well as green fee discounts. Visit www.gc2000.at for more information.

For more information on golf clubs, green fees and tournaments, contact one of these clubs:

- Club Danube Golf-Wien (22nd District) www.clubdanube.at

- Golf Club Wien (2nd District) www.gcwien.at

- GolfRange Tuttenhof www.golfrange.at

- Golf Club Schloss Schönborn www.gcschoenborn.com

Horseback Riding

To find a riding club in Vienna or nearby, see: www.reitenwien.at

- Austrian Western Riding and Breeding Association
  www.awa.at

- Reitclub Donauhof
  This club offers riding lessons in English. Call two days
  ahead to reserve a horse. You can rent a horse to ride
  along the many bridle paths in the Prater.
  www.reitenimprater.at

- Reit und Therapiezentrum Donaustadt
  Therapeutic riding, vaulting and riding for disabled.
  www.reit-therapiezentrum.at

- Reitverein Freudenau
  Offers individual and group lessons in the Prater.
  www.rvf.at

Tennis

To find tennis facilities in Vienna, look under *Tennishallen*
and *Tennisplätze*. Most outdoor courts (*Freiplätze*) have
clay surfaces and are open only in summer. Some courts
have floodlights for late-evening games; others have
temperature-controlled covered courts for winter.
Hallenplätze are covered courts, usually with carpeted
surfaces.

Tennis Associations

- Austrian Tennis Association
  (*Österreichischer Tennisverband*)
  An umbrella tennis organization for Austria. www.oetv.at

- Vienna Tennis Association
  (*Wiener Tennisverband*)
  Coordinates tennis clubs in Vienna. www.tenniswien.at

Tennis Clubs

- Colony Club
  An international group, including many AWA members,
  meets here on Wednesday mornings for friendly
  doublesplay.
  www.colonyclub.at

- Tennis Treff Achatzi
  2, Prater Hauptallee
  +43 1 720 2070
  This quiet location in the Prater has outdoor clay courts.

- Tennis Point Vienna www.tennispoint.at

- Westside Tennis and Fitness Club
  www.fitness-center.at/westside

- Grinzinger Tennisplatz
  19, Krapfenwaldgasse 13
  +43 1 328 2318
  This facility is located in a rolling, green area and has
  many international players.

- Happyland
  Just outside Vienna in Klosterneuburg, this facility has a
  tennis school, indoor and outdoor tennis courts, soccer,
  climbing, ice skating, indoor and outdoor pools, bowling
  alley, basketball courts, exercise rooms and a sauna.
  www.happyland.cc

Team Sports

Baseball

The American International Baseball Club, affiliated with Little League International, organizes games for children ages 6 to 15 from April - June. Registration and tryouts take place during the winter. You can find registration information posted at the international schools, UNO-City and the US Embassy. Teams play on the baseball fields at the Prater. There is an Austrian baseball league with several teams in Vienna.

* Austrian Baseball Federation
  (*Österreichischer Baseball-Softball Verband*)
  www.baseballaustria.com

Basketball

School teams compete in several leagues and in international and Eastern European tournaments. For information on youth and adult basketball tournaments, contact these organizations:

* Viennese Basketball Federation
  www.basketballwien.at

* Austrian Basketball Federation
  (*Österreichischer Basketballverband*)
  www.basketballaustria.at

Cricket

The Austrian Cricket Club runs Vienna's only outdoor cricket grounds. Players (men, woman and youths) come from many nations.

- www.viennacricketclub.net

- www.austriacricket.com

Flag Football

The speed version of American football is played by youths, women and men. For information see:

- American Football Confederation Austria
  (*American Football Bund Österreich* AFBÖ)
  www.afboe.at

Field and Indoor Hockey

- Austrian Hockey Federation
  (*Österreichischer Hockeyverband ÖHV*)
  www.hockey.at

- Vienna Athletic Sport Club
  (*WAC – Wiener Athletiksport Club*)
  One of the oldest hockey clubs in Europe and one of the most successful in Austria. www.waschockey.at

- SV Arminen
  (*Hockey und Tennisanlage Waldstadion*)
  www.arminen.at

- AHTC
  Academic Hockey and Tennis Club www.ahtc-wien.at

- HC Wien
  Hockeyclub Wien www.hcwien.at

- Post SV www.postsv.com

Soccer

Soccer (*Fussball*) is probably the most popular sport in Vienna for youths, men and women. There are hundreds of amateur soccer teams and many leagues. For more information see:

- Austrian Soccer Federation
  (*Österreichischer Fussballbund*) www.oefb.at

- Vienna Soccer Association
  (*Wiener Fussball-Verband*) www.wfv.at

Volleyball

Volleyball is played at school level as well as at clubs. To find places to play volleyball, check the websites of these groups:

- Austrian Volleyball Federation
  (*Österreichischer Volleyball Verband*)
  www.beach.volleynet.at

- Beim Matsumae Budo Center www.budocenter.at

- Beachvolley Club - Wien Alte Donau

Austria's largest beach volleyball club directly on the Danube. Recreational players as well as top Austrian players, Beach Cup players and young talent can be found here. www.beachvolleyclub.at

To locate a club in your area and for more information see: www.beachvolleywien.at/locations

Climbing

* Austrian Alpine Association
  (*Österreichischer Alpenverein*)
  The climbing center is open to non-members. Members pay reduced fees. They organize trips and sell equipment and clothing. www.alpenverein.at

* Kletterhalle Wien
  The largest indoor climbing facility in Austria, with rental equipment available. www.kletterhallewien.at

For a list of other climbing (*Klettern*) locations: www.wien.info/en/vienna-for/sports/climbing-walls

Hiking

Hiking has a long tradition in Vienna. Popular destinations include the vineyards and wine taverns (*Heurigen*), the Vienna Woods (*Wienerwald*), and the Lainz park (*Lainzer Tiergarten*). Vienna's Forestry Office has laid out 16 hiking trails (*Wanderweg*) that take you through beautiful scenery in and around Vienna. The *Stadtwanderwege* (city hiking paths) are equipped with directional arrows. Except for city hiking path 1a, all paths run in a clockwise direction. For a list of city hiking paths and information, visit: www.wien.gv.at/english/leisure/hiking

Many books with information about hiking (*Wandern*) as well as route maps for hiking tours throughout the Austrian Alps are available in English. *Walking Austria's Alps* by Jonathan Hurdle and *Walking Easy in the Austrian Alps* are recommended.

For information on hiking in the Alps see:
Austrian Alpine Association (*Österreichischer Alpenverein*) www.alpenverein.at

You can purchase maps and books, including *Die Alpenvereinshütten*, which includes addresses, telephone numbers, hut hours and other useful information.

Nordic Walking

One of the most popular sports in Austria, Nordic walking simulates cross-country skiing. Take a brief lesson to learn how to walk correctly with Nordic walking poles for maximum benefits. You can find Nordic walking information at www.bewegdichgesund.at or www.nw-wien.at

Running

There are many running (*Laufen*) paths within the city, in parks and along the Danube. A brochure in English with information about several organized runs is available at the City Info office at city hall (*Rathaus*). The Vienna City Marathon is usually held in April or May. The *Frauenlauf*, an annual 5K and 10K run and Nordic walk for women, is held in late spring.

- Vindobona Hash House Harriers
  VH3 is an international running group that meets weekly at different Vienna locations for a non-competitive cross-country run followed by a beer social.
  www.viennahash.at

Water Sports

Both the Alte Donau, a series of lakes to the north of the main Danube stream, and the Neue Donau on the north side of the Donauinsel, are good for paddleboats, kayaks, sailboats, rowboats and windsurfing. Boat rental (*Bootsvermietung*) is available at:

- Bootsvermietung Alte Donau Irzl www.alte-donau.info

- Marina Hofbauer www.marina-hofbauer.at

Sailing

You can sail (*Segeln*) on the Alte Donau in Vienna and on the Neusiedlersee in Burgenland, about 30 kilometers from Vienna.

- Austrian Sailing Association
  Österreichischer Segelverband
  www.segelverband.at

- Vienna Sailing and Windsurfing School
  Segel- und Surfschule Wien
  This school offers sailing and windsurfing lessons in
  English as well as sailboat, motorboat, rowboat,
  paddleboat and windsurfer rental.
  www.segelschule-wien.at

- Schule Hofbauer
  This school offers instruction in sailing and windsurfing
  for adults and children on the Alte Donau and at
  Neusiedl am See. Instruction in English can be
  arranged; call at least two weeks in advance. You can
  rent sailboats if you have sailing experience.
  www.hofbauer.at

Scuba Diving

Even though Austria is land-locked, you can still learn how
to scuba dive (*Tauchen*).

- Scuba Schools International Austria
  The USI offers inexpensive diving courses in their
  swimming pool. Theory and practical skills are taught to
  beginners. Rental equipment, air and air fills are
  included in the price. www.uni-tauchen.at

- CMAS Diving Center www.diving.at

Swimming

Vienna has many public indoor and outdoor swimming pools
with qualified lifeguards. Some older pools are
architecturally interesting including *Jörgerbad* in the 17th
District and *Amalienbad* in the 10th District. Vienna's

outdoor swimming pools and beaches on the Alte Donau are open from May to September. Brochures on Vienna's pools are available at the City Info Office (*Stadtinformation*) at city hall (*Rathaus*), or see the city website: www.wien.gv.at/freizeit/baeder

You can swim in the Danube in bathing areas along both banks of the Neue Donau. For locations, see: www.wien.info/en/vienna-for/families/outdoor/danube-island

To get to the New Donau, take the U1 to Donauinsel, and walk until you see the crowds. Nude beaches are located at both ends of the Donauinsel.

To find an indoor pool in your district, see: www.wien.gv.at/freizeit/baeder/uebersicht

To find an outdoor pool near you, see: www.wien.gv.at/english/leisure/bath/

Waterskiing

Most of Vienna's waterways are protected by environmental regulations however there are a few open-water areas where waterskiing is permitted.

* Wasserskilift Neue Donau
  In summer, a rectangular draglift pulls you over the water for about one kilometer at speeds between 28 to 58 kilometers/hour. www.wakeboardlift.at

Windsurfing

The Donau and Neusiedlersee are good places for

windsurfing. Here's where you can find information on lessons and equipment rental.

- Firma Ing. Wolfgang Irzl
  Offers windsurfing and sailing lessons
  22, Florian-Berndl-Gasse 33-34
  +43 1 203 6743

- K. Hofbauer Sailing School
  Segelschule Hofbauer
  Group and private lessons for men, woman and teens
  www.hofbauer.at

Winter Sports

Cross-Country Skiing

The city of Vienna opens its cross-country ski (*Langlauf*) trails when there is at least 8 inches (20 centimeters) of snow on the ground. Designed for both beginners and experienced cross-country skiers, the eight groomed cross-country trails (*Loipen*) are accessible by public transportation. For more information see: www.wien.gv.at/freizeit/sportamt/arten/

- High Hills
  Hohe-Wand-Wiese www.highhills.at

You can also find cross-country skiing trails at these locations:

- Prater   2nd District
- Wienerberg   10th District

• Steinhofgründe	14th District
• Schwarzenbergpark	17th District
• Cobenzl	19th District (ski rental available)
• Donauinsel	21st and 22nd Districts
• Maurer Wald	23rd District

Ice Skating

In Vienna, the season for ice skating (*Eislaufen*) runs from mid-October to mid-March. These are the main ice skating organizations and rinks in the city:

- Vienna Ice Skating Society
  Wiener Eislaufverein www.wev.or.at

- Wiener Eistraum
  At Rathausplatz from late January to early March. Skate and locker rental available. www.wienereistraum.com

- Wiener Stadthalle www.stadthalle.com

- Kunsteisbahn Engelmann (17th District)
  www.engelmann.co.at

- Albert-Schultz Eishalle (22nd District)
  The home of the Vienna Capitals ice hockey team.
  www.albertschultzeishalle.at

Skating in Nature

In addition to skating rinks, there are lakes and ponds in and around the city.

- Ausstellungsstrasse (2nd District)
- Osterleitengasse (19th District)
- Hanselteich (Vienna Woods)
- Alte Donau
- Schloss Laxenburg
- Neusiedlersee in Burgenland

Skiing and Snowboarding

There is a ski area in Vienna's 14th District, the *Hohe Wand Wiese*. For information see: www.highhills.at

Travel agencies, sporting goods stores and local newspapers have information about bus trips to nearby ski resorts, including Semmering, Stuhleck and Hochkar/ Lackenhof.

Here are a few of the many websites where you can find information and make travel bookings for Austrian winter sports:

- www.austria.info/us/tags/ski-snowboard
- www.ski-austria.com
- www.bergfex.com/oesterreich/top10

Snowshoeing

You can go snowshoeing (*Schneeschuhwandern*) in and around Vienna on the hiking trails in the *Wienerwald*. Or try the trails at Raxalpe, south of Vienna. Some Nordic walking instructors offer classes and guided snowshoeing tours in the winter. See www.nw-wien.at. The VIC Hiking Club also organizes snowshoeing hikes.

Tobogganing and Sledding

You can go tobogganing or sledding (*Rodeln und Schlittern*) on hills in Vienna's parks. For a complete list of sledding hills, see: www.wien.gv.at/umwelt/parks/anlagen/rodel.html

You can also toboggan at many ski areas. Be aware that tobogganers and skiers may compete for slope space, making for a sometimes crowded and unpredictable adventure. In the Prater, kids can slide down a 30 to 60 meter long slope from a ten-meter-high sledding hill. To find out whether the snow conditions are sufficient for sledding, call **+43 1 4000 97200**.

Sports and Recreation for Seniors

These sports facilities have special classes and times for seniors:

- Brunswick Bowling
  Special prices for seniors
  2, Praterhauptallee 124   +43 1 728 0709
  17, Schumanng. 107   +43 1 486 4361

- Tanzschule Stollhof
  Dance classes for over 50. www.stollhof.at

- Kunsteisbahn Engelmann
  Special skating times for seniors. www.engelmann.co.at

- Wiener Eislaufverein
  Senior skating sessions. www.wev.or.at

- Swimming pools (*städtischen Schwimmbäder*) have special swim times and prices for seniors. For more information see: www.wien.gv.at/freizeit/baeder

- Tennisanlage Hrubesch
  Offers reduced senior rates. www.tennishrubesch.at

- Vienna Fitness and Sport Association
  (*Wiener Arbeiter Turn- und Sportverein WAT*)
  Fitness classes and sports teams for members over 50
  12, Sagedergasse 10
  +43 1 804 8532

Sports and Recreation Glossary

ace (tennis)	das Ass
advanced	fortgeschritten
backhand	die Ruckhand
bicycle	das (Fahr)Rad
bike rental	der (Fahr)Radverleih
bike trail, lane	der (Fahr)Radweg
cross country skiing	das Langlaufen
cross country trail	die Loipe
daily pass	die Tageskarte
exercise equipment	die Geräte
horse	das Pferd
hunting license	die Jagdkarte
indoor (tennis) court	die Halle
instructor	der Trainer
jump rope	das Seilspringen
map	der Plan, die Karte
martial arts	der Kampfsport
member	das Mitglied
membership	die Mitgliedschaft
muscle	der Muskel
nutritional advice	die Ernährungsberatung
rowing machine	die Rudermaschine
session, lesson	die Stunde
ski slope	die Piste
stationary bike	das Zimmerfahrrad

steam room	das Dampfbad
strength training	das Krafttraining
tennis court	der Tennisplatz
tennis racquet	der Schläger
tennis serve	der Aufschlag
to become a club member	in einem Club Mitglied werden
to bicycle, to go by bike	radfahren
to book, reserve a lesson	eine Stunde buchen
to dive	tauchen
to go horseback riding	reiten
to go sled riding	schlittern
to go snowshoeing	schneeschuhwandern
to go to the gym	ins Fitnesscenter gehen
to go tobogganing	rodeln
to hike	wandern
to hunt	jagen
to ice skate	eislaufen
to rock climb	klettern
to run	laufen
to sail	segeln
to serve (tennis)	aufschlagen
to ski, go skiing	schifahren
weight loss	das Abnehmen

In Case of Emergency

FIRE   122
POLICE   133
AMBULANCE   144

EUROPEAN
EMERGENCY NUMBER 112

18. IN CASE OF EMERGENCY

Emergency Telephone Numbers

Fire Department	Feuerwehr	122
Police	Polizei	133
Ambulance	Rettung	144
Poison center	Giftzentrale	+43 1 406 4343
Hearing Impaired *Accepts SMS messages*	Gehörlose	0800 133 133
European Emergency Number *from all phones in Europe*	Notfall	112
Air ambulance	Aertzeflugambulanz	014 0144
Auto assistance	ARBÖ ÖAMTC	123 120
Child services	Kinder- und Jugendanwalt	080 024 0264
Crisis hotline	Telefonseelsorge	142
Dentist	Notzahnarzt	+43 1 512 2078 141
Doctor	Notarzt	141
Electricity	Stromstörung	080 050 0600
Highway emergency	Autobahn-Notruf	+43 1 172 0
Mountain rescue	Bergrettung	140
Natural gas	Gasgebrechen	128

Pharmacist	Apothekenbereitschaft	1550
Plumber	Installateur	+43 1 586 3730
Police station	Polizeidienststelle	059 133
Prescription delivery	Medikamente-Lieferung	+43 1 891 44
Psychiatric hotline	Psychiatrische Soforthilfe	+43 1 313 30
Sewage line	Kanalgebrechen	+43 1 400 0930 0
Taxi companies	Taxi	+43 1 31300 +43 1 40100 +43 1 60160
Veterinarian	Tierarztnotdienst	+43 1 531 16
Water	Wassergebrechen	+43 1 599 590
Women's Hotline	Frauennotruf	+43 1 717 19
Youth Hotline	Rat auf Draht	147

Emergency German

Although most emergency services have English speakers, here are phrases and words in German that you may want to know.

Do you speak English?	Sprechen Sie Englisch?
I need a doctor.	Ich brauche einen Arzt.
I need an ambulance.	Ich brauche einen Krankenwagen.
My name is . . .	Mein Name ist . . .
My address is . . .	Meine Adresse ist . . .
accident	Unfall
aches	Schmerzen
ambulance	Rettung
appendicitis	Blinddarmentzündung
asthma	Asthma
bleeding (severe)	Blutung (starke)
breathing difficulties	Atemnot
burn	Verbrennung
emergency	Notfall
fever	Fieber
fire	Feuer
handicapped	behindert
handicapped accessible	behindertengerecht
head injury	Kopfverletzung
headache	Kopfschmerzen
heart	Herz

heart attack	Herzanfall
hemorrhage	Blutsturz
migraine	Migräne
muscle soreness	Muskelkater
nausea	Übelkeit
pain	Schmerzen
poisoning	Vergiftung
serious accident	schwere Unfall
severe pain	heftigen Schmerzen
unconscious	bewusstlos
vomiting	Erbrechen

We hope you've enjoyed *Living in Vienna.* To learn more about AWA Vienna or to join, please visit our website.

An International Community
of English-Speaking Women

The American Women's Association of Vienna
Singerstrasse 4/11
1010 Vienna
Austria
+43 1 966 2925
awa@awavienna.com
www.awavienna.com